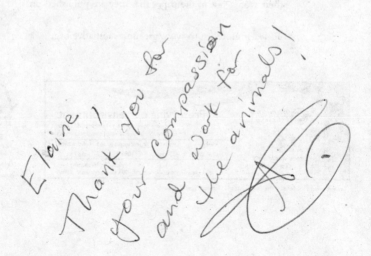

Elaine!
Thank you for
your compassion
and work for
the animals!

ANCIENT FOREST FRIENDLY

13 trees were saved for our forests

Preserving our environment

Lantern Books chose to use recycled paper to print this book and saved these resources[1]:

energy	water	greenhouse gases	solid waste
9 million BTUs	4559 gal.	1098 lbs	585 lbs

Printed by **Webcom Inc.**
on Legacy Trade Book Natural 100% post-consumer waste.

[1]Estimates were made using the Environmental Defense Paper Calculator.

FSC

Recycled
Supporting responsible use of forest resources

Cert no. SW-COC-002358
www.fsc.org
© 1996 Forest Stewardship Council

STRATEGIC ACTION
FOR ANIMALS

✳

*A Handbook on Strategic Movement Building,
Organizing, and Activism for Animal Liberation*

✳

MELANIE JOY, PH.D., ED.M.

*For Chi-Chi (2000–2008), who proved that you don't
have to be human to be a person.*

And for those whose vision helps the rest of us to see.

Lantern Books ● New York
A Division of Booklight Inc.

2008

Lantern Books

A Division of Booklight Inc.

128 Second Place

Brooklyn, NY 11231

Printed in Canada.

Library of Congress Cataloging-in-Publication Data

Joy, Melanie.

Strategic action for animals : a handbook on strategic movement build-ing, organizing, and activism for animal liberation / Melanie Joy.

     p. cm.

Includes bibliographical references.

ISBN-13: 978-1-59056-136-2 (alk. paper)

ISBN-10: 1-59056-136-8 (alk. paper)

1. Animal rights movement. 2. Animal rights activists. 3. Animal rights. 4. Animal welfare. I. Title.

     HV4708.J68 2008

     179'.3—dc22

                                    2008006166

Acknowledgments

✳

This book is the product of many contributors. I want to thank Carolyn Zaikowski and Chris Logue, who put countless hours of work into the shaping of the book; Aimee Houser, whose editorial brilliance inspired and guided me; Martin Rowe, for his patience and guidance; Bonnie Tardella, for her diligence and insights; Erik Williams, for his love; Herb Pearce, for keeping me grounded; Janice Goldman, for carrying hope; Michael Greger; Zoe Weil; George Lakey and the folks at Training for Change; Teri Jessen; Susan Solomon; Steve Bernstein; Pamela Dein; George Bournakis; Hillary Rettig; Dina Aronson; Adam Wake; Anna Meigs; Karla Koebernick; Ruth Tedaldi; the staff of the 1369 Café; Bonnie and Perry Norton; John Adams; Stephen Cina; Ngaio Schiff; and the rest of my friends and family who have supported me in more ways than I can name.

Contents

✳

Introduction

✳

Strategize, Organize, Mobilize!
How Strategy Can Empower the Animal Liberation Movement

The only sure weapon against bad ideas is better ideas.
—A. W. Griswold

IT's BEEN SAID that if you can imagine it, you can achieve it.[1] Chances are, you *can* imagine a world in which animals no longer suffer at human hands: you can imagine animal liberation. But imagining your goal doesn't guarantee that you'll reach it, or that you'll reach it as quickly and effectively as you want to. Imagining where you want to be is important, but it isn't enough. You need to know *how* to get there. You need a map, to show you the most direct route to your destination. And that map is strategy.

When you imagine animal liberation, you naturally imagine that the animal liberation movement has succeeded. You imagine that the movement has become more powerful than those it's fighting, that the majority of the public has become aware of the reality of animal exploitation and supports the goals of the movement. This shift in the balance of power is the goal of all social change efforts, and so the purpose of strategy is always to strengthen the movement.

The animal liberation movement already has some valuable strengths. Activists are often exceptionally committed to the cause: they are impassioned, energetic, and willing to stand up for what they believe in despite overwhelming pressure to conform. And the number of animal protection organizations continues to grow, with groups becoming more diverse and able to attack animal exploitation on multiple fronts and from every angle. Perhaps the greatest strength of the movement, though, is that it speaks to core human values. The vast majority of people don't want to see animals suffer, much less know that they participate in such suffering. In many ways, animal liberation is aligned with the deepest values held by most Americans, even though they may have not yet made the connection between their values and the rights of animals.

However, the industries that exploit animals are growing at a faster rate than the movement, even though the movement has probably prevented animal exploiters from doing even more damage than they could have. In the U.S. meat industry alone, ten billion animals are slaughtered every year, a significant production increase over past years[2] and which cannot be accounted for simply by human population growth. This should come as no surprise, as animal exploiters have vastly more money, influence, and proponents than animal liberationists.

Given this tremendous imbalance of resources, what's an activist to do? How can the animal liberation movement make the most of what it has so that its power is greater than that of animal exploiters? The answer is strategy. When you are strategic, you capitalize on your strengths, turn your weaknesses into opportunities, and create a force that attracts people to your side and away from those you are fighting. When the playing field is not level, strategy is the great equalizer.

Animal exploiters may have more resources, but they are no more capable of strategizing than you are, and they are aware of this truth. Industries that exploit animals employ highly trained strategists to work on all levels of the trade. But unfortunately, most activists have received less training than they would to work a cash register. This strategic differential makes it seem as though activists are fighting unarmed in a battle against a military giant. To shift the balance of power, you need to be strategically educated and trained like your opponent.

The purpose of *Strategic Action for Animals* is to provide you with the principles and practices of strategy so that you can make the most of your efforts. *Strategic Action for Animals* presents a *comprehensive strategic approach* to animal liberation, in that it provides guidelines for strategic action on all levels: movement building, organizing, and individual activism. *Strategic Action for Animals* outlines the necessary components of a strategic movement and describes a movement's natural developmental process so that you can understand how you impact the broader movement and choose your actions accordingly; it explains how to build a strategic organization, become a powerful, charismatic organizer, and avoid some of the most common and destructive pitfalls of animal liberation organizations; and it describes ways to effectively advocate to others and to cultivate a sustainable life as an activist. A comprehensive strategy can prevent some of the most debilitating problems that plague the movement: dissidence among organizations and activists, inefficient campaigns, wasted resources, and high rates of burnout.

Whether you feel that your activism is productive, destructive, or somewhere in between, strategy can help you to have more of the kind of impact you want on the lives of animals, and on yourself. And as each individual becomes more strategic, so does the movement. Imagine if every activist were to become twice as effective. The movement's power would double. Strategy has the potential not only to double but to *exponentially* increase your effectiveness, which would significantly empower the movement. If you can imagine it, and you can strategize, you *will* achieve it.

Part I

❋

Strategic Movement Building
for Animals

1

✳

Tipping the Scales
Building a Strategic Movement for Animals

*All truth passes through three stages: First, it is ridiculed;
Second, it is violently opposed; and Third, it is accepted as self-
evident.*—Arthur Schopenhauer

THINK GLOBALLY AND act locally. You've heard this motto countless times, seen it on bumper stickers, buttons, and brochures.
And it remains the guiding principle for a strategic movement
for animals: keep in mind the goals and needs of the larger
movement as you work on the task before you, so that your
actions support the movement. Activists must consistently make
the connection from the micro to the macro, considering how
the actions of an individual, an action, a campaign, an organization, or a "sub-movement"—such as the anti-fur movement—
will affect the overall movement. The lesson of think globally, act
locally, is that your individual actions will have a ripple effect on

the movement, for better or worse. A strategic movement for animals is one in which all of its parts work together, and it is united rather than divided.

Defining the Movement

In order for the parts to unify, activists must come to agreement on a common purpose and shared goals. One of the most divisive issues in the movement is disagreement about what ends activists should be working toward and how to bring these ends about. These disagreements run the gamut from which issue is most pressing to whether activists should work toward reform or abolition. What all these approaches have in common, though, is the objective of making the world a better place for animals, which means liberating animals from human oppression. From this angle, the debate is really about *degree*—how much and what forms of oppression we should be fighting. For the purpose of creating an inclusive and clearly defined movement, we can say that the objective of the movement is animal liberation, whether that means liberating pigs from confinement in gestation crates or from slaughter for human consumption.

The Goal of the Movement

While the ultimate goal of the movement is animal liberation, another goal exists alongside it. Understanding this parallel goal can give activists a shared sense of direction. For any social movement, this goal is *to become more powerful than those it is fighting*. Indeed, the goal of all movements is to transform power dynamics: to increase the power of the movement and decrease the power of the opposition. This goal is achieved when empowerment and liberation replace privilege and oppression.

A movement has three potential means for achieving this end: money, weapons, or people. It is impossible to acquire enough money or weaponry to overpower the oppositional forces—and in the case of military power, it's also unethical. The third potential choice, though, is what makes up the power base of a democratic society. It is "people power." Without the compliance of the public, the powerholders—those making decisions about how animals are treated—wouldn't be able to prevail. The more people a movement has marshaled, the more powerful it is.

The animal liberation movement therefore needs to raise public awareness so that citizens become mobilized to demand change. When the movement reaches critical mass, the balance of power shifts and the scales of justice tip. In other words, if animal liberation is to succeed, its goal must be to win popular support. When this happens, majority opinion becomes aligned with the goals of the movement instead of the opposition, and what was originally considered common sense (e.g., eating animals) becomes questioned and rejected.

Opening and Closing the Gap

Strategist Bill Moyer and others point out that the way to win over the public is to continually highlight the gap between powerholders' policies and practices, and the social values they claim to respect. Powerholders spend a great deal of effort presenting themselves as upholding values that align with the majority of society, when in fact their practices violate these values. For instance, officials in animal agribusiness claim that the industry is committed to animal welfare. They go to great lengths to promote this myth, realizing that most Americans wouldn't willingly support extensive animal cruelty. It is vital for the animal liberation movement to uncover and expose the secrets of powerholders, and raise public awareness through all viable means, from education to civil disobedience.

Highlighting the hypocrisy of powerholders decreases *their* power, but it doesn't automatically increase the power of the movement. The movement will only increase its own power when it bridges the gap between public perception of the movement and the values the movement stands for.[3] In other words, activists must make the case that it is the movement, not the powerholding elite, that truly reflects social values.

Americans profess a deep commitment to democracy, freedom, honesty, and justice. The animal liberation movement must appeal to these values—and demonstrate that animal exploitation violates them—in order to close the gap. The movement cannot do this if it positions itself as the enemy of the mainstream, even though activists understand that their goal is to oppose the status quo. And the opposition holds onto its power by presenting an image of the movement and of activists as militant, extremist, totalitarian (trying to rob consumers of their freedom to choose), and anti-American. To appeal to the general public, then, the movement has to reflect the values and speak the language of the people it is trying to attract. It has to position itself as mainstream.

Mainstreaming a Radical Movement

When a movement is considered radical, it simply means that its views fall outside those of the majority. However, many activists overvalue radicalism and disdain anything they consider a compromise. Some disdain compromise because what attracted them to the movement in the first place was their perception of it as inherently radical, as positioned against *something*. For others, it is simply because they believe that mainstreaming means selling out and giving up their deepest convictions.

But mainstreaming the movement doesn't mean changing the movement's values. It means framing or presenting them in a way that speaks to the people it is trying to attract. The movement has to "sell" its values to the majority, which means presenting itself in a way that those outside the movement can relate to. It can only achieve this through a commitment to non-violence, in the tradition of Mahatma Gandhi and Martin Luther King Jr., and a commitment to transparency, or being upfront and honest about its motives and actions. The goal is to juxtapose the violence and secrecy of those who exploit animals with the opposite practices of the movement. At the same time, activists must do everything in their power to come across as conventional as possible. If the aim is really to liberate animals, and not to gratify our own egos, we must be willing to wrap ourselves in the garb of the mainstream.

Nonviolence

If you've been involved in the animal liberation movement for any period of time, no doubt you are aware of the controversy about whether it's appropriate to use violence as a tactic. While it's true that acts of violence can sometimes offer short-term gains—as when burning millions of dollars of laboratory equipment causes a company that uses vivisection, or animal experimentation, to lose time and money—from a strategic perspective, violence is fundamentally counterproductive for several reasons. I'll discuss the specific tactical problems caused by violence in Chapter 5; here, the focus is on the ways violence weakens the movement as a whole.

The core demand of the animal liberation movement is that people refuse to participate in acts of violence, from eating meat to buying products that have been tested on animals. How can activists hope to have this demand taken seriously when they engage in acts of violence themselves? Moyer et al. point out how, even if violence is carried out in the name of saving lives, the general public, uninformed about the issue and already skeptical of animal liberation, will see activists who perpetrate it as villains rather than heroes, as hypocrites rather than advocates. The activists seem no different from those they are rallying against, acting as though any means justify their ends. And powerholders, who control much of the media and therefore determine how an action is framed for the public, are aware of this perception and use it to pull public support away from the movement and toward themselves. Violence not only turns people off to the cause, it also deflects attention from the real victims, the animals. And it makes the entire movement seem dangerous—especially if there's been violent police intervention in an action—which can scare off otherwise sympathetic supporters.

Transparency

Transparency means being as honest as possible with the public and with others in the movement about your intentions and actions; it is the opposite of secrecy. Transparency doesn't require exposing all campaign strategies, but rather openly discussing your beliefs, motives, objectives, and—unless it's absolutely necessary to keep them classified—your plans. Strategist George Lakey argues that, while secrecy is necessary in totalitarian regimes, in a democratic society "underground organizing is a strategic disaster."[4]

Secrecy makes it look like activists have something to hide. If activists truly believe in the rightness of their choices they should demonstrate this belief by not keeping their actions hidden. Open rescues are an excellent example of transparency: activists enter a facility and free the animals that are being exploited in plain view. Often they will even notify the media to publicize their actions.

Secrecy also provides a breeding ground for *agents provocateur*, opponents of the movement who masquerade as supporters in order to infiltrate and weaken it. *Agents provocateur* can harm the movement in different ways: they can incite violence during demonstrations, giving police an excuse to use violence against protestors; they can acquire and expose confidential information; and they can encourage activists to question and turn against one another. Secrecy creates the perfect climate to foster suspicion and distrust among activists and between activists and the public. Transparency protects against these problems, as it creates an atmosphere of openness and trust because activists don't have anything to hide.

What this all comes down to is that, in a strategic movement for animals, activists have to represent the kind of change they are trying to bring about in society. They, and the organizations they represent, are ambassadors for the movement, for better or worse.

Roles of Activists and Organizations

Moyer et al. developed a revolutionary model for understanding how social movements evolve over time. Central to this model is the idea that movements contain different types of activists and organizations that work simultaneously and in different roles, including: the Citizen, the Rebel, and the Reformer. These roles can be played effectively or ineffectively. Problems arise when activists don't play their roles effectively, or when they devalue the roles other activists play.

The Citizen is the upstanding member of society, the one to whom the mainstream can easily relate. For example, humane educators and welfare organizations like the SPCA are Citizens: they use conventional tactics and language to promote their message. The Reformer may or may not be more radical than the Citizen. What distinguishes the Reformer is that he or she typically works in a professional opposition organization, an organization of professionals working within the movement, such as the Physicians' Committee for Responsible Medicine (PCRM) and the Animal Legal Defense Fund (ALDF). Reformers help mainstream the movement by giving it professional representation, as when medical doctors argue that animal products don't belong in the Food Guide Pyramid or psychologists claim that cruelty to animals is a symptom of psychological disturbance. The Rebel is more confrontational, participating in rallies and perhaps civil disobedience. Though the tactics of the Rebel are more radical, his or her self-presentation still has to appeal to the mainstream. In the animal liberation movement, the first two roles are more often played effectively, while the Rebel is often (though certainly not always) played ineffectively. An effective Rebel enables the public to bear witness to the issues at hand, while an ineffective Rebel is volatile, angry, anti-American, dogmatic, and fringe. He or she tends toward reactivity, implementing tactics without thinking them through. The ineffective Rebel typically burns out quickly and does a major disservice to the movement. An example of a Rebel organization is People for the Ethical Treatment of Animals (PETA); many of its actions have been effective, but some have not.

A strategic movement for animals contains all three types of activists and organizations; each plays a different yet vital role in the growth of the movement. When activists accept that all roles are valid and important, the movement will be more unified and therefore much more powerful.

The Evolution of a Movement

Changing people's attitudes and behaviors toward humans is difficult at best, and changing the way people relate to animals is even harder. The goal of the animal liberation movement is to subvert centuries of deeply ingrained beliefs about the role of animals in society. It challenges thousands of years of tradition as well as enterprises that have a combined worth of trillions of dollars.

If you're a new activist, you probably expect that education is the key to liberating animals. Many new activists (and sometimes more seasoned activists) expect that when people learn about the atrocities inflicted upon animals, they will change their behaviors immediately. And while some people do, most do not. Most people need to be persuaded over time, as new ideas require time for discussion, reflection, and, eventually, integration.[5] Those activists who stopped supporting exploitative institutions once they became aware of the truth are especially prone to frustration and even despair in the face of what seems like irrational or selfish resistance.

A strategic movement for animals is one in which activists realize that all movements evolve through a predictable series of stages that unfold over the course of decades. This realization provides a powerful antidote to despair, and it also enables activists to develop strategies that are appropriate to the particular stage of the movement.

Moyer and others determined that there are eight stages in the evolution of a movement, each stage having its own goals, and that the movement is made up of a variety of sub-movements, which may exist at different stages of development at any given time. The success of a movement is dependent on the combined successes of its sub-movements, and the strategy of a sub-movement has to be connected with the overall goal of the movement. For instance, while the vegetarian movement is working to abolish meat consumption, and the anti-vivisection movement is working to end animal experimentation, both these sub-movements are ultimately working toward the broader goal of animal liberation and their strategies have to support this.

In Stage One, the majority of the public doesn't know the problem exists and/or supports the institutions that are the cause of the problem, seeing the views of the movement as radical and often ridiculous. The goals of this stage are to recognize and document that a serious problem exists that violates societal values, to identify powerholders and their role in sustaining the problem, and to create various groups and infrastructures to oppose oppressive institutions. In Stage Two, the goal is to prove to the public that institutions and powerholders perpetuate the problem. Activists must try to resolve the issues through all official channels, such as courts and governmental offices, so that when these channels fail to provide satisfactory resolution, the movement will have demonstrated that the broader social system actually prevents the democratic process from working. For example, if your organization petitions a District Attorney's office to have a scientific researcher charged with animal cruelty and the petition fails, you will have shown that the legal system protects the scientists, rather than the animals. While Stage Two can be frustrating, as activists' actions seem to make little concrete difference, its combined efforts lead to Stage Three, in which the movement grows exponentially. In this stage, many new activist groups emerge, and the public becomes increasingly aware of and concerned with the issue. But Moyer et al. caution that, in order for a movement to reach this stage, the public must also be more distrustful of powerholders in general, a factor that isn't in activists' control.

At the end of Stage Three, a single "trigger event" occurs that sets off a visible, national campaign of rallies and other actions, catapulting the movement into public awareness—as when the arrest of Rosa Parks ignited the civil rights movement. The trigger event ushers the movement into Stage Four. While powerholders work to keep people misinformed and denounce the movement, the movement's focus is on winning greater public support and creating a political platform to prepare for future legislative changes, though few actual legislative changes take place during this stage. Eventually, the momentum of Stage Four dissipates, and the movement appears to be petering out, which can lead activists into despair. From Stage Four, there are three possible directions the movement can go in: it can move into Stage Five (which Moyer et al. call "Perception of Failure") and die, as activists give up; it can move through Stage Five into Stage Six; or it can go directly to Stage Six.

Stage Six is less visible than Stage Four but it's no less powerful. In this stage, the focus is on working for policy changes and continuing to win greater public support. "Re-trigger" events in Stage Six are not uncommon. Many powerholders will proclaim that the movement is dead in order to dissuade activists and the public from continuing to support it. But other powerholders will start to fight among themselves about how and to what degree the demands of the movement should be met. During this stage, the issue becomes controversial in all sectors of society.

In Stage Seven, official policies and laws are replaced by those that originate out of the movement. Sometimes this happens over decades, and the movement isn't given credit for the changes. Activists can then despair and quit, thinking that their actions haven't made a difference. However, Stage Seven can lead into the final, Stage Eight, in which reforms grow into true social transformation. Though Stage Eight may seem like an endpoint, activists need to continue pushing forward throughout this stage in order to protect the movement from being weakened by a *backlash*.

Backlash

A backlash is a social reaction against a movement, brought about by powerholders in an attempt to win back power. A backlash is actually a sign of progress; it means the movement has gained enough strength to truly pose a threat to the powers that be. Social change is an ongoing process of progress/backlash/ progress.

The most common and effective method of disempowering a movement is to "shoot the messenger." If you discredit the messenger, you don't have to take seriously his or her message. This strategy most often takes the form of promoting negative stereotypes of activists, such as those of the overly emotional animal-lover or the angry human-hater. Such stereotypes suggest that the movement is irrational and hostile to "outsiders," place the focus on distorted images of activists while detracting attention from the real issue, denigrate the emotionality of what is essentially an emotional issue, and can shame activists into silence by making them feel hypersensitive.

Debunking negative stereotypes is vital for the success of the movement. It is another example of why it's so important for activists always to model the values they are trying to instill in society, such as compassion and integrity. And once the backlash has been managed, the movement finds true success. Then the movement's message, which was first seen as ridiculous and then violently opposed, has become accepted as self-evident. It has won.

2

＊

One Struggle, One Fight?
Human Freedom Is Not *Animal Rights*
(And Why This Matters)

It is wisdom to know others; it is enlightenment to know oneself.—Lao Tzu

ANIMAL LIBERATION IS *not* human liberation. Though all liberation movements are interconnected in many ways, assuming that working for animal liberation is the same as working for human liberation, just with different victims, is one of the gravest mistakes activists can make. Not appreciating the uniqueness of the animal liberation movement causes two serious problems: despair that can lead to burnout, and strategic errors.

There are three key features that distinguish the animal liberation movement from most other movements: the scope of institutional and personal investment in maintaining a speciesist status quo is unparalleled by any other form of exploitation in human history; animals cannot advocate for themselves, and so a powerful source of testimony and witnessing is missing; and animals are legal property, rather than legal persons, which seriously limits activists' ability to use legislative channels to work for change. For these reasons, changing attitudes toward animals is significantly harder, and thus slower, than changing attitudes toward humans. However, if you recognize these issues, you can be prepared to work around and against them.

The Scope and Power of Speciesism

The animal liberation movement is fighting what is arguably the most entrenched and widespread form of exploitation in human history: speciesism. Every major institution endorses speciesism, including education, medicine, science, nutrition, government, and entertainment. And virtually every human being benefits directly from the use of animals: animal products comprise much of what people eat, wear, and use for personal hygiene; and even animal-friendly consumers buy inexpensive materials made from animal by-products, such as glue, film, cold remedies, and cosmetics. As Peter Singer points out, not many people can view animal oppression with the detachment they may bring to other social concerns; even Northern whites could bring to the slavery question a more objective view of the issue, because they had less personal investment in maintaining the slave trade.[6]

People are also psychologically invested in maintaining speciesism. The belief in human superiority over animals is so longstanding and fixed that to suggest otherwise is to be seen as ludicrous and even offensive. Learning to view oneself as a strand in the web of life, rather than atop a hierarchical ladder of life, requires a willingness to relinquish privilege and a sense of superiority, and this is typically only accomplished with great effort. It is important to understand that change is and will be slow. It is all too easy to become demoralized and burn out because you have underestimated the magnitude of the struggle for animal liberation.

Activists as Advocates for Animals Who Cannot Advocate for Themselves

Most liberation movements have been founded by people who were motivated by self-interest, fighting for the rights of their own group. In general, the direct victims of exploitation become the activists for change, joined only later in the movement's evolution by others. And even those movements that have depended on outside advocates, such as the child protection movement and the abolition movement, were able at some point to include the voices of the victims.

Activists for animal liberation have to speak for victims who literally cannot speak for themselves. This poses a serious challenge. Direct victims have much more moral authority to call attention to their own suffering; they are often allowed and even expected to be outraged and outspoken. On the other hand, advocates of victims appear moralistic when they speak out on behalf of the victims. For instance, the public is much more sympathetic to veterans speaking about their personal experience than to antiwar activists who talk about the suffering of soldiers. When you are an advocate, you're seen as taking the moral high ground, which can cause others to feel morally inferior and defensive for not having made the same choice you did.

For this reason, it's important to frame your message as *empowering rather than blaming*. Choose to invite people into the movement as allies rather than stand apart from them as opponents. The speciesist system victimizes everyone—including humans. Humane people make inhumane choices largely because they are uninformed or have been misinformed, and are often shocked and ashamed when they realize what they've been contributing to. Nobody wants to identify with the bad guy, and people will go to great lengths to avoid seeing themselves in a negative light, including refusing to support a cause they might otherwise believe in. The general public is not the enemy; the system and powerholders are. When activists view people as compassionate and capable of being part of the solution, they are less likely to come across as moralistic and condescending.

The Property Status of Animals

Under United States law, one can be classified as either a legal *person*, or legal *property*. Legal persons are entitled to certain basic rights, such as the right to exist free from being harmed by others. Obviously such a right doesn't guarantee that a legal person will live unharmed, but this right is a mandate that can be fought for in a court of law. In contrast, the rights of legal property exist only in relation to the person who legally owns that property. Damage to property is given legal consideration only insofar as its owner has been impacted. For example, a car can't sue someone for breaking its windshield, but its owner can.

Today, all human beings are legal persons, and animals are legal property. The property status of animals is important to understand for two reasons. First, it explains why the animal liberation movement's success will be slower than that of other movements. With the exception of some environmental movements (and the anti-abortion movement), other movements have fought for the rights of legal persons, not property. Even African slaves were considered three-fifths persons. So other movements have sought to extend rights, rather than to obtain legal recognition of rights—a far less complicated process.

Second, some activists believe that one focus of the movement should be on attaining personhood for animals, because they see the property status of animals as the greatest impediment to animal liberation. If animals were persons, they would be legally entitled to protection from bodily harm. The legal personhood of animals would give activists tremendous leeway in their fight against animal exploitation.

A strategic movement for animals is one in which activists are aware of and sensitive to the uniqueness of the movement. With this understanding, they can have realistic expectations and develop appropriate strategies, both of which can significantly hasten the growth of the movement.

3

＊

Preventing Strategic Suicide
How to Resist the Divide-and-Conquer Counterstrategy

We must be together; our masters are joined together and we must do the same thing.—Mother Jones

THE FASTEST AND most effective way to kill a movement is to kill it from the inside. Powerholders know this, and employ divide-and-conquer strategies to create or reinforce divisions within a movement, and between that movement and other movements. For example, powerholders may portray some activists in an anti-vivisection demonstration as terrorists and others as reasonable moderates who want to distance themselves from the radicals. Divisions pit activists against each other so that the movement commits suicide and does the powerholders' job for them; a divided movement is disjointed and therefore inherently unstrategic. Unfortunately, many activists have already set this process in motion with infighting and a competitive attitude toward other movements.

The antidote is to recognize and counter this strategy. A strategic movement for animals is united internally as well as with other movements that are working for a more just society. In a strategic movement, activists don't work against each other, nor do they merely tolerate each other. They are mutually supportive, and in their solidarity they create the power base of the movement.

Divisions within the Animal Liberation Movement

Within the animal liberation movement, there are a variety of viewpoints on which issues should take precedence, which ideology and tactics are most appropriate, and what kind of organization (e.g., national or grassroots) is most effective. Healthy debate strengthens a movement, as it encourages activists to think through issues more fully and come up with creative, collaborative solutions. But differences of opinion become a problem when activists are dogmatic, believing that only one ideology and approach is legitimate and that others in the movement must adopt their particular method.

Dogmatism is a problem largely because activists don't appreciate that the success of the movement depends not on choosing one approach among many, but on using all of them. Strategic movements *need* a diversity of activists and organizations. A well-stocked toolkit enables activists to attack oppression from every angle and to attract a diversity of supporters. For instance, humane educators raise consciousness about the lives and deaths of farmed animals; professional opposition organizations like the Physicians' Committee for Responsible Medicine

(PCRM) prove that a vegetarian diet is healthful; and direct action organizations like Viva! organize campaigns to abolish certain factory farming practices. And each of these types of organizations appeals to different kinds of supporters. Someone who isn't attracted to a direct action organization, for example, might join a welfare group instead. Without the welfare group, that person might never have put forth an effort to help animals. Also, the success of every sub-movement contributes to the overall success of the movement, so there is no single issue that will lead to animal liberation.

Reform or Abolition? The Welfare–Rights Debate

One of the most contentious issues in the animal liberation movement is the debate about whether activists should be working toward reform (animal welfare) or abolition (animal rights). Reformists often view abolitionists as unrealistic, making radical demands that alienate the public. They argue that because animal exploitation won't end anytime soon, efforts should be directed toward reducing animals' suffering. Therefore, reformists work to abolish specific practices, such as the use of tiny and painful gestation crates that confine sows in concentrated animal feeding operations (CAFOs). Reformists also sometimes argue that welfare reforms will eventually lead to abolition. For example, creating more humane conditions for farmed animals would lead to more expense, which in turn could increase the cost of meat so that few could afford it.

Abolitionists, on the other hand, accuse reformists of selling out, being ineffective in their efforts to help animals, and even of slowing the progress of the movement by giving powerholders legislation to hide behind. They argue, for instance, that animal experimenters can legitimize themselves in the eyes of the public by citing their adherence to the Animal Welfare Act (AWA) as "proof" that they aren't harming animals.

Because animal suffering is so extensive, activists often assume this means that the movement is failing, and can blame each other. However, there are many reasons for the increase in animal suffering, from population growth to centralized power among animal exploiters. It is likely that the animal liberation movement has helped slow what would otherwise have been an even more extensive problem. Strategic movements require both reformists and abolitionists. Welfare organizations save millions of animals from abuse and abandonment, allowing more radical groups to focus on other types of work, such as direct action. And the radical stance of abolitionists makes reformists seem more mainstream, which allows them to push a less conservative agenda than they otherwise would. For instance, the Humane Society of the U.S. (HSUS), once focused solely on the protection of companion animals, can now advocate for reforms in factory farming because in comparison to abolitionist organizations their demands seem moderate. The entire movement ultimately becomes more progressive.

Internal Privilege and Oppression

Within the animal liberation movement, sexist, racist, classist, and other discriminatory attitudes are not uncommon. This creates internal divisions and also turns many people away from the movement. For instance, anti-fur campaigns that use women as sex objects to sell their message offend feminists within and outside the movement. These campaigns present the movement as hypocritical, fighting human privilege while reinforcing male privilege. Discrimination within the movement also prevents it from attaining the diversity that would give it richness and strength. For example, some activists (incorrectly) assume that people of color or people who are socio-economically disadvantaged lack the time, energy, or mindset to care about animals. This robs the movement of potential supporters and reinforces prejudicial assumptions.

Because privilege is entrenched, and invisible to those who have it, activists have to make a commitment to listening to those who are on the receiving end of discrimination, without denying or minimizing their experiences. A forum for dialogue about these issues should be built into all organizations and conferences.

When activists seriously expand their political analysis to include human animals as well as nonhuman animals, the movement will be far more appealing to activists from other movements. This will help bridge animal liberation with the other movements it is so naturally aligned with.

Divisions between Animal Liberation and Other Movements

The animal liberation movement seeks to create a world in which animals are no longer exploited by and for humans. This kind of change will not happen in a vacuum; animal liberation will likely not be realized as long as the majority of society believes it is acceptable to sacrifice the needs of those who are less powerful to serve the interests of those who are dominant—that it's appropriate for some groups to be privileged at the expense of others. Seen this way, the objective of animal liberation is aligned with the goals of many other movements. Animal, human, and environmental exploitation all fight privilege and disempowerment in an attempt to create a more egalitarian society.

However, the animal liberation movement is largely disconnected from other movements, and even competes with them for everything from resources to ideological superiority. Failing to recognize the interconnectedness of oppressions and the ways activists in the animal liberation movement actually reinforce certain oppressions that other groups are working against, is one of the reasons the movement has remained marginalized and even viewed with contempt. The movement has pushed away those who might otherwise be its closest allies. Of course, the blame doesn't fall solely on animal liberation activists; activists from all movements contribute to this competitive dynamic. But a strategic movement for animals works actively to counter these divisions.

Bridging the divide between movements means being open to and informed about issues other than animal liberation. It means recognizing that there is no *objective* hierarchy of oppressions, no matter how extensive and intensive the suffering of animals is. Suffering is subjective. Even on a purely practical level, oppressions are not linear but intersecting, as when meat production exploits animals, laborers, human consumers, and the environment simultaneously. When movements unite, they can build coalitions, share strategies, and support one another's cause. At the very least, by uniting, they won't work against each other, as powerholders would have them do.

Globalization and Unification

Economic globalization refers to capitalism on a global scale, to the developing of a single global economy. The superpowers of this economy are transnational corporations—corporations that reside in more than one country. These corporations, through a series of trade agreements and organizations, have been granted more power than national governments, which means that their interests (which are profit-driven) supersede the interests of national citizenry. One of the most serious consequences of globalization is that anything posing a "barrier to trade"—anything that makes a corporation lose profits—has been deemed illegal. Profits are lost when corporations have to respect animal welfare, human rights, and environmental protection. In other words, it has become that much more difficult, and imperative, to protect all forms of life. Economic globalization has had a devastating effect on animals, laborers, citizens, and the ecosystem and it has become the natural point of intersection for different movements.

The anti-globalization movement is made up of activists fighting for a variety of causes but with an overarching objective: to restore democracy by putting the welfare of people, animals, and the environment before corporate profits. Animal liberation activists can use the fight against economic globalization as an opportunity to support other movements while also promoting their own agenda, as all oppressions are linked within the matrix of corporate exploitation. Learning about the issues and then making an effort to connect with other activists in the fight against globalization is a logical first step and can lead to many more powerful connections.

Activists from all movements have to work alongside, rather than against, one another. A strategic movement for animals is united, internally and externally, and in this unity it finds its power.

Part II

✳

Strategic Organizing for Animals

4

❋

Strategy Is Destiny
Running a Strategic Organization for Animals

Use power to curb power.—Chinese proverb

I WAS ONCE asked to work as an informal consultant with a newly formed animal rights organization. The group had worked tirelessly to build the organization—staging demonstrations, supporting animal-friendly political candidates, and holding awareness-raising events for the community. All the organizers were seasoned activists who had been involved in animal liberation for years.

When I asked the main organizer what the focus of the organization was, he described a number of goals, from helping start a national animal rights Web-based support network to shutting down the local university's biomedical research center. But the core purpose, he said, was to "mobilize the animal rights movement in the community," which the organization intended to do through petitioning and leafleting, staging protests, and organizing teach-ins. I asked who the core organizers were, and he said the group was continually changing; there had been disagreements over everything from which issues were most pressing to how often and where to hold meetings, and they were trying to recruit new members through distributing brochures around the community.

As you may have guessed, the organization foundered and eventually disbanded. There are many reasons for this, and sadly they are not uncommon among animal liberation organizations. The group was unaware of dysfunctional power dynamics in their organization that sabotaged any effort toward progress; they lacked a clear sense of their mission; they didn't know what their organizational model or structure was; they didn't define the role(s) of the organizers—or even know who the core organizers were; they used exactly the same outreach strategies for every group, from conservative white-collar businessmen to antiwar activists; they were unwilling to work with other organizations by building coalitions; they held disorganized and/or hostile meetings that bored, confused, or even offended members; and they failed to develop a long-term strategic plan. A strategic organization for animals takes all of these issues into account.

Power and the Strategic Organization

A movement is only as powerful as its organizations. How organizations relate to power, both externally and internally, determines whether they succeed or fail.

Organizations are a microcosm of the movement, which seeks to convert social power dynamics from exploitative to democratic. The goal is to transform *competitive* power, which is the sense of power one gets at the expense of another—by wielding power over another—into *cooperative* power, which is the power that comes from helping others to attain their own power and from distributing power more equitably. Competitive power leads to disempowerment, while cooperative power leads to empowerment. For example, an act of competitive power is the trapping of animals to profit from the sale of their fur, while an act of cooperative power is the enactment of legislation that bans trapping, preventing furriers from abusing their power over fur-bearing animals.

Cooperative power has to be practiced within the organization as well as externally. Organizations that operate on competitive power are inherently dysfunctional and will inevitably fail. This isn't to say that healthy organizations don't have hierarchical reporting structures, but that the way staff members relate to one another is cooperative. Decisions aren't made unilaterally, information is widely shared, and all opinions and positions are respected. For example, leaders of an organization that operates cooperatively may decide that forming a coalition with another group would benefit a current campaign, but they would present this idea to the staff, which would then deliberate on it and help determine whether to move ahead with the plan.

Just as the movement acts as a model for the kind of society it is trying to create, so too does the organization. If your group is fighting centralized power, your organizational power must be decentralized. If your group is working to build a democratic society, your organizational culture must be democratic. It is impossible for the movement to succeed if its organizations don't reflect the principles on which it is built. The issue of power dynamics in organizations is so crucial that I have dedicated an entire chapter to it, Chapter 7. But the bottom line is that a strategic organization is a cooperative organization.

Organizational Models, Missions, and Structures

A strategic organization is clear and consistent in its *model, mission*, and *structure*. The Midwest Academy, a leading group of strategists, provides an excellent overview of these factors: the *model* should explain what kind of organization it is—educational, direct action, advocacy, legislative, or any combination of these—and what issue it's focused on, such as veganism or anti-vivisection. For example, The New England Anti-Vivisection Society (NEAVS) advocates for the protection of animals through outreach, education, and legislative initiatives. An organization's *mission* should define its purpose. NEAVS's mission is to "expose and replace animal experiments…with…modern research methods." The *structure* is the framework of the organization, and should be comprised of the *staffing patterns*, including roles of staff members, such as education director or CEO; *programs*, such as direct action campaigns and political lobbying; *policies*; and *practices*. The structure is the design that allows the organization to carry out its mission.

All three elements must be clearly defined, agreed upon by all staff, and unified. Otherwise, staff members will be frustrated and confused, and campaigns will be ineffective. For instance, if the model of an anti-fur organization is educational, in that it is focused on educating the public, but its mission is to enact legislation to ban steel leghold traps, the model (education) is inconsistent with the mission (legislative). Problems also arise when the model isn't clear to everyone involved, or it is inconsistent with the mission statement and/or not supported by the structure. Similarly, problems arise when the mission statement is unclear, or when it isn't realistic and is impossible to fulfill— as when, for example, an organization seeks to educate the community about veganism, abolish vivisection, and pass legislation banning greyhound racing. The main problem that occurs with an organization's structure is a lack of clarity around roles. Staff needs to know exactly what is expected of them and what the reporting hierarchy is. They need to know that they can do their job successfully. Often, staff members are given more responsibility than they can possibly fulfill and end up confused, disillusioned, and eventually burning out.

Strategic Organizers

Organizers are personnel in key leadership positions. Their role is to build the power base of the organization and to channel this power externally to bring about change. If you are an organizer, in order to empower the members of the organization as well as challenge external power structures, you need to have a good understanding of power dynamics. Organizers who don't recognize this need are not only less effective, they are counterproductive, as they disempower staff and decrease public support through running campaigns that damage the reputation of the organization and the movement.

Strategic organizers have a set of characteristics and skills that make them effective. Renowned organizer Saul Alinsky says that strategic organizers display the following traits and behaviors: they avoid dogma and remain open to others' ideas while maintaining faith in their own position; they are realistic yet optimistic, so that people have hope and reason to fight for change; they help people recognize their own power to bring about change; they continue to learn new skills to enhance their leadership and organizational abilities, such as conflict resolution and new tactical strategies; they stay focused on goals and make sure others do the same; and they maintain a sense of humor to keep up morale. Organizer Lee Staples points out that leaders must present issues in a way that makes sense to people's understanding of power; telling people to "take back the power" or saying "power to the people" makes no sense to people who don't understand how power is personally and socially wielded. Furthermore, effective organizers must have excellent communication and facilitation skills. They should listen more than they speak and communicate directly and clearly to constituents as well as powerholders. They should also share information freely, so that others are groomed to step into positions of leadership if necessary and so their knowledge doesn't die with them, leaving others to waste precious time reinventing the wheel. In a nutshell, strategic organizers model the values and practices they are working to bring about in the world.

Target Groups and Outreach Strategies

A target group is a group toward which an organization conducts outreach. The most effective way to attract supporters is to target those groups that are most likely to join your organization and then tailor outreach strategies specifically for them.

Many animal liberation organizations fail to tailor their outreach strategies and lose countless potential supporters. They try to attract supporters by using a blanket outreach approach, targeting every group at once and using the same language and tactics for all audiences. For instance, most vegetarian organizations use the "three-pronged" approach to attract anyone their message can reach: they promote vegetarianism based on animal welfare concerns, environmental preservation, and health—the assumption being that most people will be motivated by at least one of these arguments.[7] This would be like Toyota using only one advertisement to attract teenaged girls, middle-aged businessmen, and new parents. Instead, companies like Toyota conduct analyses to determine who is most likely to buy a product, and then develop a different advertising campaign for each demographic. Activists in animal liberation organizations need to develop a similar approach, determining who is most likely to support an issue and then tailoring their message for that constituency.

Finding Potential Allies

An excellent method for determining which groups to target is called the Spectrum of Allies. This exercise helps organizers decide which groups are most and least likely to support them, and which ones fall in between. The goal is to create a diagram in which a detailed spectrum of supporters becomes clear: allies, opponents, and neutral parties. Specific instructions are in Appendix 1.

Potential allies will vary from organization to organization. However, there are several groups that are likely targets for any animal liberation organization: human rights/peace organizations; certain religious groups, such as Quakers, Unitarian Universalists, Buddhists, Hindus, Jains, and progressive branches of Christians, Jews, and Muslims; environmental organizations; and other animal groups, such as rescue organizations and wildlife protection centers. (See www.lanternbooks.com/readings

for a list of readings on this subject and of organizations that are potential allies.)

Reaching out to Potential Allies

One of the reasons organizers fail to recognize obvious allies is because they assume that the ideological differences between their groups are greater than their similarities. These organizers operate under a scarcity model, assuming that others are in competition with them for scarce resources, including supporters. The first step in reaching out to would-be allies, then, is to view them as natural supporters rather than potential competitors.

To reach out to potential allies, you need to become familiar with the culture of the target group. Doing so helps you understand the ways the group's ideology overlaps with animal liberation, and it also makes it possible to tailor your message for that group. For instance, when talking to a Buddhist, you should refer to basic Buddhist tenets such as nonviolence and compassion for all beings; and when advocating to a Quaker you should connect animal liberation with peace, justice, and conscientious objection. Alinsky says that you should also dress and act in accordance with the norms of the group you're reaching out to, so that your message is more likely to be heard. You can learn about the principles and practices of other groups by reading about them, attending their meetings, and talking to other animal liberation activists who have worked with these groups.

Some of these target groups already have branches that are working on animal liberation, such as Jews for Animal Rights. They may also have members who are supporters of animal liberation but haven't yet started a branch within their group to focus on this. So, finding out who is doing what in target groups is a logical first step. As with all strategy, start with what's closest to you and work your way outward from there.

Recruiting and Retaining New Members

There are a number of methods with which to conduct outreach, such as canvassing, leading awareness-raising workshops or lectures, networking at local or national conferences, fundraising, conducting public or open meetings, and holding movie screenings. However, the Midwest Academy points out that, regardless of the method, people will only become involved in a cause if the benefits of doing so outweigh the costs. Organizers need to be sure they make joining the organization as attractive and empowering as possible, which means creating an organizational culture that cultivates dynamic, inspired, and empowered members rather than one full of infighting, confusion, and embittered, burned-out activists. The Midwest Academy also says that *joining the organization* shouldn't require *quitting one's life*—activism isn't an all-or-nothing occupation. If people choose to dedicate their free time to a cause, facing potentially traumatizing issues for no monetary compensation, then membership has got to be more attractive than staying home and relaxing.

For the benefits of membership to outweigh the costs, you have to appeal to people's self-interest and make sure the process of working with the organization isn't discouraging. Some aspects of membership that appeal to members' self-interest include socializing with like-minded people, developing skills for a career, and simply adding some excitement to life. Members can also cultivate personal development, as participation in the organization gives them a chance to act in accordance with their deeper values.

New members are often discouraged by organizational practices that could have been avoided. People need to be given something engaging to do so that they can feel useful; they need to be included in conversation and not confused by jargon and concepts that they aren't familiar with; and they need to be welcomed into the group and appreciated for their efforts, by being greeted and introduced to others and thanked for their participation with a follow-up phone call or e-mail. Most importantly, they need to understand how their contribution is making a difference. Knowing how to appeal to potential members requires listening to them. Strategic organizers never assume that what motivates them will motivate another. They listen to people and determine what those individuals need in order to feel inspired, and they respond accordingly.

Building Coalitions

A coalition is an alliance between two or more organizations. It can be temporary, focused on a specific campaign, or permanent. Coalitions can significantly empower an organization, but they can also cause serious problems. The union among organizations should be thought of as a union among individuals: if it is mutually beneficial and cooperative, the relationship is greater than the sum of its parts; if not, it disempowers all parties.

In a cooperative coalition, organizations are focused on the goal of winning a campaign, rather than promoting their own ideology. They also don't pressure more conservative groups into using radical tactics and they don't squeeze out smaller groups by denying them equal say or failing to credit them for their contributions. Cooperative coalitions operate like cooperative organizations; they are simply larger systems.

Working with Labor Unions

Many animal liberation organizations make the egregious strategic error of disregarding the power of labor unions to affect their campaigns. Organizers fail to consider the impact their campaigns will have on workers, and end up provoking Labor. And when Labor is opposed to a campaign, activists will have to work significantly harder to reach their goals. Therefore, it's actually less important to understand how to work *with* Labor than how *not to work against* them.

For example, in Massachusetts in 2000, activists launched a major campaign to ban greyhound racing in the state. They had worked for years, petitioning legislators, staging demonstrations, leafleting, collecting signatures across the state, advertising in the newspaper and on the subway and television, making bumper stickers and T-shirts——and they even hired a professional consultant and attorneys. On top of this, Massachusetts is a historically liberal state. Yet, despite all they had going for them, when the issue went to the polls, the activists lost by a two percent margin.

One reason the bill wasn't passed was that the racetrack owners outspent the activists on advertising. However, the campaign might still have been successful if Labor hadn't opposed it. Labor unions, fearing massive layoffs of racetrack workers, organized against the campaign and swayed the vote. Labor hung its own banners and staged its own protests, arguing that banning greyhound racing was bad for workers and their families. Had the activists been aware of this issue, they could have approached union leaders with proposals for alternative solutions, such as including in their campaign a demand that workers be adequately compensated for layoffs or that dog racing be phased out over a number of years. They could also have conducted their own research or hired a neutral third party to do so, in order to get an accurate number of how many union jobs would actually be lost, since the statistics presented by racetrack owners were likely skewed. Even if Labor had still decided to act against the campaign, the activists could have dialogued with union *members*, rather than *leaders*, to sway the labor majority opinion. It is not unheard of for union leaders to accept financial incentives from businesses in order to get their members' support for a particular issue, and union leaders are often the members' sole source of information about an issue. The activists could have tried to appeal to the membership despite the stance of its leaders.

It is understandable that animal liberation activists tend to diminish the impact their campaigns will have on workers. In the face of the horrific circumstances of the animals, layoffs seem trivial. But the threat of unemployment is not trivial to the people whose livelihoods are at stake. Activists need to learn to truly listen to the concerns of the workers and, as social educator Griff Foley points out, not minimize the reality of the situation by arguing, for instance, that their jobs will be obsolete in several years anyway. Workers are concerned with their immediate situation, not with a hypothetical future.

While it's essential not to work against Labor, working with Labor can be of tremendous benefit to activists. Labor unions are powerful, well organized, and skilled in strategic activism, and can lend support to animal liberation organizations in these areas. Also, by supporting the fight against the oppression of workers, activists are helping fight the same system that oppresses animals. In *Organizing for Social Change*, The Midwest

Academy offers some excellent suggestions for working with Labor and I highly recommend reviewing that information.

Holding Strategic Meetings

Strategic meetings are effective meetings, and they are fundamental to the success of an organization. They reflect the values, dynamics, and structure of your group, and they will either inspire and retain members or disenchant and lose them. Meetings are also where vital decisions are made, and they therefore need to be structured so that organizational choices are as strategically sound as possible.

One of the last animal liberation meetings I attended was for a medium-sized group that had been active for a couple of years. During the meeting, I was struck by the disorganization, lack of focus, and conflicts that arose from inadequate planning and structuring. The meeting started almost a half hour late, because people continually trickled in; the agenda covered more issues than we could adequately discuss in five meetings, let alone one; and, when the meeting was supposed to end, the organizers disregarded the time, continuing to read down agenda items. I had another meeting to attend, but I didn't want to appear rude by leaving in the middle of the discussion, and I felt trapped and frustrated by the organizers' lack of respect for others' time. Moreover, only the most aggressive participants spoke (often, but not always, these were men), even when the whole group was asked their opinion on a major decision, while the more timid members sat by silently. By the time the discussion finally ended, I felt exhausted, uninspired, and unclear as to what the actual mission of the organization was or what my role with them should be.

The organizers of these meetings were some of the most dedicated activists I had known. They simply were unaware of the basic principles for holding strategic meetings. The following guidelines would have helped them immensely, and of course they apply to all meetings:

- Make sure meetings are focused on important organizational issues, such as the organization's strategic plan or managing dysfunctional power dynamics, rather than on simply brainstorming or making announcements.
- Clearly state the goals of the meeting, and make sure these goals are attainable.
- Don't hold meetings more often than absolutely necessary.
- Never hold meetings that last for longer than two hours.
- Plan out agendas beforehand, don't time them to the minute so that there's no room for flexibility, and make sure they're in writing.[8]
- Start and end meetings on time. If certain issues don't get addressed, plan for a follow-up meeting to discuss them.
- Be clear about who will facilitate, who will keep time, and who will take minutes to keep in the organization's archives and to distribute to participants as soon as possible after the meeting has ended.[9]
- Whenever possible, arrange chairs in a circle so that all participants can see each other.
- Make sure that participants are clear about what is expected of them after the meeting.[10]
- Respect and show appreciation for participants' time and energy: thank them for coming, ensure that they are properly greeted and introduced to one another, offer them

refreshments, and make sure they feel that their efforts make a difference.

- Seat people in the front rows so the room doesn't look empty and people aren't scattered among empty seats.

Meetings are only as effective as the person who facilitates them. A skilled facilitator is able to create an empowering group dynamic that stimulates creative thinking and inspires members to act. The facilitator should model the kind of dynamic he or she wants to create in the meeting. Following are guidelines for strategic facilitation:

- Look at everyone in the room when you speak.
- Make sure to give everyone a chance to speak and prevent individuals from dominating the conversation.
- Rephrase soft or unclear comments people make so that everyone can hear and understand them.
- Listen more than you talk.
- Keep the conversation focused by guiding people who stray off topic back to the agenda.
- Pay attention to the emotional climate: if there is tension in the group, address it before moving on. For example, members might be feeling demoralized after a failed campaign, and need to discuss this before they can be open to new ideas. Acknowledge the emotions, but don't get bogged down by details.
- Don't let people discuss the animal suffering they've witnessed. If they do, the meeting can veer off task and other group members can become traumatized.
- Never criticize people's ideas. If their comments are in con-

flict with the goals of the group, find something positive to say about them while gently pointing out that they might not fit in with the current goals. Also, try not to let participants criticize each other, even if it's in subtle ways such as rolling their eyes or sighing.

- Aim for consensus whenever possible. Otherwise, if decisions are made based on the majority vote, make sure that those who disagree are still willing to support the decision. People need to feel that they have a voice, even (or especially) if it's in the minority.

- At the end of the meeting, summarize what was said, focusing on the positive.[11]

- Identify and defuse power struggles with *nonviolent conflict resolution* techniques.

Nonviolent Conflict Resolution

When handled appropriately, conflict can offer opportunities for personal and organizational development. It can also be a sign of growth; conflict can emerge as a person (or group) struggles to assimilate a new way of thinking that has challenged the boundaries of their existing one. To increase the likelihood that conflict is productive rather than destructive, the basic guidelines apply:

- Highlight common ground, the areas in which people do agree.

- Make sure that all parties feel that their concerns are heard. Restate their position clearly and respectfully.

- Maintain open body language and eye contact.

- Show your own vulnerability so that the others feel less

threatened showing theirs. For instance, share your own feelings of having been in a similar situation.

- Avoid black-and-white thinking. There is no clear-cut good and bad; acknowledge that there is truth on all sides and, even if you strongly hold one position, there are aspects of the other side that can be considered. Validate both sides of the argument.

- Focus on the behaviors, or ideas, rather than the character of those in conflict. Good people can have ideas that others see as bad; this doesn't make them bad people.

- Be clear about what each party needs in order to feel the issue is resolved.

- Look for solutions that are win–win, rather than win–lose, and consider that there might be an alternative solution to those requested by either side.

- Be as impartial as possible; never take sides.

- Get to the root of the problem. Sometimes a deeper issue, such as a power struggle, is being expressed as a particular conflict.

- Make sure that, when wrapping up, you summarize the situation and everyone is satisfied with the agreement. Commend people on their willingness to work through conflict.

Conflict resolution, like other practices we've discussed, is an important skill to help transform discord into harmony. This skill is essential, because like a strategic movement, a strategic organization is internally and externally unified. A strategic organization promotes and achieves unity among the staff, among elements of the organization, and with other organizations.

Developing a Long-term Strategic Plan

Developing a long-term strategic plan—or an organizational plan—is the most important project of any organization, as it ensures that members are working toward the fulfillment of the organization's mission. It gives a clear sense of direction, acting as a roadmap to reaching the organization's goals. However, many organizers fail to develop this plan, largely because they think the process is abstract and complicated. While developing an organizational plan does take time, it is in fact quite straightforward.

A long-term strategic plan is a series of steps, each building on the one before it, that leads to the goal(s) of the organization and, ultimately, the movement. Strategists Kehler, Avazian, and Senturia have put together an excellent guide for developing a long-term strategic plan, *Thinking Strategically*, which informs much of this section.

Developing an organizational plan takes time and should not be rushed. It needs to be accepted and understood by everyone involved, and it has to be realistic. This section presents the steps in developing your plan.

Plan to Plan

Many activists are resistant to developing long-term strategic plans. Often, the magnitude of the suffering they are working to relieve makes anything that won't bring about immediate results seem fruitless. According to Kehler, Avazian, and Senturia, activists also resist planning because they have a variety of unfounded fears of the process, such as the fear of compromising creativity and flexibility, and the fear of failure.

Regardless of the reasons, if you don't address the resistance in your group it will be impossible to move forward. Once you understand the planning process, you can set up a meeting to discuss it with staff and discuss any resistance that arises. When everyone is on board, the next meeting can be set up to discuss the basics of planning. You should start by asking the following questions: What is our group's overall mission? Where are we now in relation to our mission? Where do we want to be in two, three, five, and ten years? How do we get there from here?

Developing an organizational plan takes weeks or even months. Meetings to discuss the plan should be held on at least a weekly basis. You should get as many people to participate in developing the plan as possible, even if this means distributing questionnaires among the membership to determine what they think about the organization and what they believe its focus should be.

Define the Mission

A clearly defined mission is essential to developing a sound strategic plan. Make sure that the mission is realistic, clearly stated, agreed upon by all staff, and supported by the structure of the organization.

Define Organizational Goals

The goals of the organization need to be stated explicitly and accepted by staff. Your goals also need to be measurable, so that you can determine when you have reached them. For example, "raising public awareness" is vague and impossible to measure, while "replacing animal laboratory experiments with humane alternatives" produces visible and measurable results.

The Midwest Academy says that organizations should have three categories of goals: *long-term*, *intermediate*, and *short-term*.

Long-term goals are aspects of the mission. For example, if your mission is to replace animal experiments with alternatives, your long-term goals might include getting medical and/or veterinary schools to allow students to opt out of animal experimentation. You should also clarify when you hope to achieve these goals, even if it will take ten years. *Intermediate* goals are the goals won by specific campaigns to help you reach your long-term goals. For example, passing legislation granting medical and veterinary students the right to refuse to dissect or vivisect animals would be an intermediate goal. *Short-term* goals are steps toward your intermediate goals. For instance, a short-term goal might be obtaining enough signatures to get the proposed "students' freedom to choose" bill on the ballot.

Kehler, Avazian, and Senturia say that there are three other types of goals as well: *external program* goals, *internal organizational* goals, and *community outreach* goals. *External program* goals are goals that affect the world outside the organization, such as allowing students to refuse to experiment on animals. *Internal organizational* goals impact the organization itself, such as doubling membership or creating a funding program. *Community outreach* goals impact those you want to attract to your organization through outreach. For example, you might have as a goal recruiting university students.

Each of these goals reinforces the others. Once you are clear about your goals, you are ready to analyze the current state of affairs of your organization and community.

Assess the Starting Point: Determine the Internal and External State of Affairs

Determining the internal and external state of affairs is like looking at a map that says, "You are here." It helps you gain a clear understanding of who and what your resources are, as well as who and what are working against you. There are several ways to figure out where you stand. One that I mentioned in Chapter 4 is creating a Spectrum of Allies chart. Some other methods include developing a Force Field Analysis and creating a SWOT Analysis.

Force Field Analysis

A Force Field Analysis is a diagram that helps organizers determine which forces are working for them and which are against them. It focuses on all factors that will help or hinder the organization's mission and goals. For example, returning to the New England Anti-Vivisection Society (NEAVS) mission, which involves replacing animal tests with humane alternatives, the forces working *against* the mission include pro-vivisection propaganda, and the public's ignorance about vivisection and fear of compromising important medical advances for human beings. The forces working *for* the mission include people's natural tendency to care about the welfare of animals and the growing base of companies that have been moving toward alternative research models. The Force Field Analysis should be used as an accompaniment to the Spectrum of Allies. A sample diagram is presented in Appendix 2.

SWOT Analysis

A SWOT Analysis is a tool that helps organizers determine the Strengths, Weaknesses, Opportunities, and Threats that pertain to their organization. A SWOT Analysis can be used after a Force Field Analysis to separate the information into *internal* and *external* issues. *Internal* issues are the organization's strengths and weaknesses, and *external* issues are opportunities and threats from the outside that affect the organization. The purposes of the SWOT Analysis are threefold: first, to understand the state of affairs regarding the organization and its environment; second, to determine how to build on its strengths and opportunities; and third, to convert weaknesses and threats into strengths and opportunities. For example, you might use your diverse membership (strength) to attract more supporters (changing weakness into strength), or you may approach a newly appointed legislator (opportunity) with an animal protection bill. A detailed explanation and a sample SWOT analysis are given in Appendix 3.

Create a Time Line for Your Strategic Plan

Kehler, Avazian, and Senturia say that, after determining what your organization's goals are and analyzing what obstacles lie in the way of reaching them, it is time to create a time line: a series of steps with a time frame for each of them. You should use a single time line for each goal, estimating how long you think each step should take and then doubling that estimate. Following are some guidelines for creating a time line:

- Determine the necessary steps to reach each goal: short-term, intermediate, and long-term.
- Estimate how much money, staff and volunteer time, and other resources will be necessary for each step.
- Estimate how long each step will take.
- Write the plan and time line for each goal on a separate chart.
- Put the strategic time lines together to create a consolidated, multi-goal time line. This way people can see how the goals and strategies fit together into one plan.

For example, NEAVS might have a time line that looks like this:

Mission: to replace vivisection experiments with alternatives.

Long-term goal: getting medical and veterinary schools to allow students to opt out of animal experiments.

Intermediate goal: passing state legislation that grants medical and veterinary students the right to refuse to experiment on animals.

Short-term goal: obtaining enough signatures to get the proposed bill on the ballot.

Strategic steps:

- Make a Spectrum of Allies chart.
- Develop a Force Field Analysis.
- Conduct a SWOT Analysis.
- Contact other groups that are working on the same or similar issues, to collaborate.
- Develop and conduct outreach strategies for specific groups that would support the campaign.
- Start collecting signatures to support the bill.
- Design educational materials to circulate.
- Develop public awareness-raising strategies (leafleting, workshops, etc.).
- Develop strategies to defuse counter-campaigns by the opposition.
- Send the bill to the legislature for consideration.
- Continue a massive outreach effort to mobilize the public to contact representatives in support of the bill (stage regular demonstrations and hold vigils in front of the Statehouse and/or laboratories where animal experimentation is taking

place, etc.) and make sure the media is informed of these actions.

● Leaflet outside all polling places on Election Day.

Kehler, Ayvazian, and Senturia recommend that once long-term goals have been broken down into intermediate and short-term goals, which have themselves been broken down into steps, each step should then be broken into a series of projects, or *tactics*. A tactic is a specific action that enables completion of a step. You should create a specific plan with a time line for each tactic, and appoint separate committees for each one. The plan should include all of the following:

● The specific activities used for each tactic.
● When each activity must be completed.
● Who is in charge of carrying out the activity.
● How much each activity is likely to cost and how money will be raised, if needed.

Kehler, Ayvazian, and Senturia also say that activists need to be accountable for their progress and the plan itself needs to be continually monitored, so it's essential that organizers develop a system of evaluation. Evaluations should include a review of the progress of each person's work and of the overall plan. This way, you can catch problems before it's too late, making adaptations when and where necessary, and group members can stay on track. Evaluations can be done on a biweekly or monthly basis.

A strategic plan helps to create a strategic organization, and a strategic organization is a powerful organization. Since organizations comprise the power base of a movement, a strategic organization for animals helps build a powerful movement for animals—and will ultimately lead to animal liberation.

5

✳

Engaging the Peaceful Warrior
Waging a Strategic Campaign for Animals

Power concedes nothing without a demand. It never did and it never will.—Frederick Douglass

THE YEAR 1977 marked the first significant victory in the history of the anti-vivisection movement, which had existed for over a century without stopping a single experiment. The campaign, run by activist Henry Spira, succeeded in ending experiments on mutilated cats at the American Museum of Natural History and was such a triumph that it mobilized the modern animal rights movement.

Spira's campaign was as strategic as it was successful. Spira carefully planned each action so that it fit into the bigger picture of the campaign and the movement. Yet he was also adaptive, staging moves and countermoves in response to the actions of his opponents. All the while, Spira communicated his message to

56

the public and the media in a way that ensured popular support. The campaign was like a chess game: Spira had a clear objective, an understanding of the rules and framework of the game, and knowledge of the key players and the power they and he wielded. He also anticipated his opponents' moves and changed course when necessary, without warning and without compromising his strategic plan. Spira understood that checkmating the opponent was the way to win the game.

What Is a Strategic Campaign for Animals?

A campaign is an *organized effort* made up of *progressive steps* to win a *measurable goal*.[12] It is focused on a specific issue, with a specific goal—or demand—made of a specific target (person or persons). For instance, Spira's campaign issue was a research project that used live cats for experimentation, a species he knew would elicit public support, and his goal was to force the lead researcher to end the experiments.

A strategic campaign like Spira's requires following progressive steps: conduct research to determine which issue is most appropriate; choose the issue; choose the target(s); conduct research on the target(s), the institution, and on the state of affairs that affect your campaign; frame the issue for the public and powerholders; open communication with the target; announce the campaign publicly; and develop tactics. Depending on the campaign, some of these steps may be interchangeable. When you develop your campaign plan, which is the same as the long-term organizational plan we discussed in Chapter 4, only applied to campaigns, you can determine what sequence of steps makes sense to you.

Jim Schultz, founder and executive director of the

Democracy Center, an international agency that trains citizens in strategic organizing, suggests using nine questions to develop a strategic campaign:

- What do we want? (What are our goals?)
- Who can give it to us? (Who has the power to meet our demands?)
- What do they need to hear? (How can we frame our message to reach the groups we are trying to move, including our opposition?)
- Who do they need to hear it from? (For example, do we need experts to vouch that an experiment is ineffective? How should we present ourselves to the public and power-holders?)
- How can we get them to hear our message?
- What resources do we have? (What are the past campaigns we can refer to, alliances we can build, etc.?)
- What are our weaknesses that we need to strengthen?
- How do we begin? (What short-term goals can we define?)
- How can we tell if it's working? (How can we evaluate and measure our progress?)

These questions don't invoke hard-and-fast rules. Rather, they are intended to help guide you as you develop a long-term strategic campaign plan.

Direct Action Organizing

The type of campaign your organization will run depends on its model. For instance, a service organization such as an animal shelter might use fundraising campaigns. But because animal exploitation is institutionalized, in that it is accepted and promoted by all major social institutions, activists often can't turn to existing power structures for support. Therefore, many animal liberation campaigns will use *direct action*. Direct action focuses on achieving a specific goal by challenging existing power relationships. In other words, every tactic focuses on increasing the power of the campaign while decreasing the power of the opposition.

Power relationships shift when organizers deprive the other side of something they want, as when Spira deprived the museum of members and benefactors; they give the opposition something it wants, such as offering public support to a company that bans cosmetic testing on animals; or they get an official who supports the issue elected. Also, power is built over time; early campaign tactics exert less pressure than later ones.

Choosing an Issue

Spira didn't choose to focus on the museum's cat experiments simply because he felt moved by the issue. He had researched a number of issues to determine which would be most strategic. The issue he chose met the criteria he needed: it was a specific experiment, it was winnable (failed campaigns can diminish activists' morale and discourage public support for the issue), it was appealing to the public, and it was non-divisive, in that it didn't alienate a significant segment of the public, as the campaign to ban greyhound racing did when it provoked Labor (discussed in Chapter 4).

When deciding which issue to choose, you should find out what other animal liberation organizations are working on, to possibly join their campaigns or build on them. It's also a good idea to consider what issues are currently in the public spotlight.

For instance, if incidences of cruelty toward animals in zoos have recently been exposed, a related issue like canned hunts might be an effective area of focus. The key is to find an issue that has enough weak links so your campaign can effectively disable it—and finding that issue requires research. I highly recommend learning more about conducting research, as it can make or break a campaign. (For further resources see www.lanternbooks.com/resources.)

Choosing a Target

The target is the person (or sometimes persons) who is in a position to meet the demands of the campaign. The target has to be a person, because human beings, not institutions, make decisions and have feelings that can be appealed to. And supporters won't feel the same outrage toward an abstract entity such as an institution as they will toward a person. Spira, for instance, specifically targeted the lead researcher, Lester Aronson, and to some degree Aronson's assistant, rather than the museum.

To determine the best target for a campaign, you need to research all possible targets. One thing to find out is what institutional body owns or funds the one you're targeting, and who the key decision-makers are. Often there are a number of people who could be targets; the deciding factor should then be who is most vulnerable. Once you've settled on a target, he or she will probably try to shift responsibility to others, and it can be difficult to determine who is to blame. While a number of people probably do share responsibility for the problem, don't let them endlessly pass the buck. Be prepared for evasive maneuvers, and pick one target to pin down or "freeze" so that your campaign will have the focus it needs.

After choosing a target, you should learn everything about that person's vulnerabilities and strengths, as well as who is allied with and opposed to him or her, and what conflicts exist within the target's group, since capitalizing on such conflicts can weaken the target.[13] You should also learn whether any of the target's values differ from those of the institution, so you can use this discrepancy to appeal to his or her sense of integrity.

If efforts to pressure the target are unsuccessful, you will have to find another target. This person, the *secondary target*, is someone who has more influence over the first target than you do, and is someone over whom you have more influence than you had over the original target. You would pressure the secondary target into pressuring the primary target. The secondary target has to be a power holder; it can't, for example, be an administrative assistant, since such a person doesn't have enough influence over the primary target. For instance, when Aronson wouldn't comply with his demands, Spira targeted the president of the museum Board of Trustees.

Framing the Issue

You communicate your message every time you discuss or present the issue, for better or worse. Framing the issue means delivering your message so that your audience hears and responds to it as you want them to. Framing the issue involves how your message is presented in campaign slogans and advertising campaigns, and it is necessary to frame the message differently for different audiences.

To frame the issue, you have to understand whether your audience is aware of the issue, what they think and feel about it, what their values are, and what they might be willing to do about it. You can answer these questions by, for instance, distributing surveys, conducting focus groups, or reviewing research that other groups have conducted. Two excellent books you may want to review for framing issues (and working with the media, which I'll discuss later in this chapter) are *Move the Message*, by Josephine Bellaccomo, and *Making the News*, by Jason Salzman. Following are some general guidelines for strategically framing the issue:

- Always keep in mind how what you say will affect your audience.
- Contrast the current conditions of animals with their natural and/or healthy conditions. For example, show an elephant in a zoo next to a free-roaming one.
- Let your audience "feel" your message. For instance, present a steel leghold trap that's used for trapping animals for fur, and use a stick to set it off.
- Don't insist that people have to believe in the equality of animals in order to support your campaign.[14] People don't have to agree that animals and humans are equals in order not to want them to suffer.
- Make sure your message is short and clear.
- Don't leave the audience feeling guilty and/or helpless.
- Never moralize.
- Avoid words that have negative connotations in the mainstream, such as *radical*, *revolution*, and *abolition*.
- Don't overload people with graphic imagery or they may become defensive and tune out.
- Don't exaggerate, or promote your own opinion; stick to the facts.
- Analyze what identity your campaign might be challenging,

and counteract it. For example, you can counteract the male meat eater's tendency to see meat as a source of strength and virility by presenting images of a powerful vegetarian male, as the hero who refuses to conform and who defends those in need of protection.

- Don't present all-or-nothing options. For instance, people shouldn't feel they have to go vegan or even vegetarian to make a difference.

Framing the Issue for Anti-meat Campaigns
Additional guidelines apply to anti-meat campaigns:

- Understand that meat eaters are highly defensive. Frame them as allies, victims of a system that withholds information from them to get them to participate in something that may be antithetical to their own values.

- Portray meat consumption as frivolous. For instance, contrast the consumer's desire for a pepperoni pizza with the suffering of pigs in Concentrated Animal Feeding Operations (CAFOs).

- When campaigning against meat, focus on animal welfare. The health and environmental consequences of meat production are easily debatable.

- Empower people. Even if an individual can't change the system, he or she can change his or her relationship to it—and to himself or herself. And in the process, though they can't save everyone, they can certainly save some animals.

Framing the Issue for the Opposition

Framing the issue for the opposition requires a slightly different strategy. Following are guidelines:

- Determine what the target stands to lose or gain from conceding to your demands. Frame the message positively, highlighting how the benefits of giving you what you want outweigh the costs. For example, if your campaign is against a cosmetics company that tests on animals, point out how they will improve their public image by conceding to your demands or lose consumer support by refusing them.

- Try to have fallback demands in case your original ones aren't met.

- Be prepared for the target's arguments and have a plan to rebut them.

- Listen to the target's concerns and look for win–win solutions; be willing to compromise. Spira says that if you go into a negotiation expecting all or nothing, you'll likely end up with nothing.

- Highlight the targets' own values and use their own words.[15] For instance, when Spira first approached museum officials he discussed their accountability to the public and the responsibility of researchers not to give science a bad name by carrying out useless experiments.

- Highlight what you have in common.

Strategic Tactics

I once worked with a group that was running a campaign to get a department store in the downtown area of a small city to stop selling fur. They conducted weekly and sometimes daily demon-

strations outside the store, leafleting around the entire downtown area, and they even staged a sit-in in which a handful of
them were arrested. However, the campaign never took off
because the activists had spent all of their time coming up with
one tactic after another without considering how each tactic fit
together to put increasing pressure on their target and build their
power as a group. Developing tactics in isolation from a strategy
is one of the most common mistakes activists make, and it spells
death for a campaign.

Tactics—the specific actions that fulfill the steps of a campaign—are like moves in a chess game. Each one needs to bring
you closer to checkmating your opponent, beginning with less
threatening moves and increasing pressure over time. Tactics are
comprised of moves and countermoves. For example, Spira started out trying to negotiate with museum officials. He wrote them
a letter, and called to set up a meeting. They refused to respond.
Spira's countermove was to go public with this information,
damaging the museum's reputation by exposing officials' refusal
to dialogue with a concerned citizen about a serious issue.

Another way to think of strategic tactics is through what
Gene Sharpe, who is perhaps the foremost expert on strategic
nonviolence, calls *political jujitsu*, which is using the opponents'
own power against them. The system of power will inevitably
turn on itself if you trigger it, since the system is built on the
need to dominate others. For example, you could boycott some
corporations but not others within the same industry, which
would lead to increased competition among companies, as some
capitalize on the boycott.

Finally, tactics must be nonviolent. In Chapter 1, I pointed
out that violent tactics can scare people away from joining the

movement and also portray activists as hypocritical and dangerous. Violent tactics are not strategic for other reasons as well:
when fighting a system of oppression, the opposition will always
have more ammunition than activists, so it's impossible to compete in the arena of violence; and violence gives powerholders an
excuse to use violence and extreme repression against activists.

Following are guidelines for developing strategic tactics:

- Tactics should be outside the experience of your target(s)
  but within the experience of your members. The target
  should be kept off-guard by being faced with the unexpect-
  ed, while members need to fully understand what they are
  going to do and why.[16]
- Tactics should not go on for too long. Otherwise, activists
  will get bored and lose motivation and the tactics will no
  longer be outside the experience of the target.
- Tactics should be enjoyable.
- Tactics must always clearly communicate your message to
  the public.
- Tactics should incorporate the opposition's reactions. For
  example, if an organizer is mistreated or sent to jail, this can
  be used to highlight the repressive reaction of the opposition and the organizer's willingness to suffer for the cause.
- Tactics should be archived and compiled so that other
  organizers can draw on them in the future.

Examples of Nonviolent Tactics
There are countless tactics you can implement. An excellent list
of them is in Gene Sharpe's *The Methods of Nonviolent Acton.*

Following are a few examples of these nonviolent tactics, tailored for animal liberation campaigns:

Methods of Protest, Persuasion, and Non-cooperation

- Make public speeches. For example, you can stand on a corner atop a milk crate and make a speech, as Malcolm X often did.

- Write letters to anyone who has the power to publicize or respond to your message, from editors to politicians.

- Circulate petitions, particularly those from voters in the district of a public official just before an election. With any petition, signatures should be mostly from those who have power to influence the target, such as consumers of a particular company's product. Petitions should always be photocopied before being given away and officials to whom they are given should be aware that the signatures were collected by a well-organized group and that signers will be informed of the officials' response.[17]

- Stage demonstrations in which you may march from one place to another. Signs and chants should include a positive alternative to the problem so the public can see the possibility of change. Strategist George Lakey says demonstrations should put the opposition in a bind such that it must make a choice between using repression to stop the demonstration, which allows activists to garner sympathy, and leaving the demonstration alone, which allows activists to educate the public. Also, you should view police officers as victims of the same system you are fighting, and make an effort to inform the police of your cause, intentions, and commitment to nonviolence. Police officers are thus forced to support the demonstration or violate their own principles. Police officers are not the enemy; historically, they have supported movements with which they have sympathized.

- Act out the issue in public (referred to as *street theater*). For instance, place an activist in a restrainer used by vivisectors.
- Destroy your own property. For instance, you can burn goods in a bonfire, such as products that were tested on animals.
- Stage public teach-ins to educate the public about the issue.
- Stage a boycott of a secondary target. For example, you might boycott a grocery chain that sells meat from a particular production plant, or a bank or government agency that funds the plant.
- Compel people to witness the issue, such as plastering posters all over town. Forcing people to witness violence can, however, be counterproductive, as they may become traumatized and displace their anger onto activists.
- Clog the system. For instance, Martin Luther King Jr., when under threat of being sent to prison, had people intentionally get themselves arrested to overflow the jails and paralyze the system. You can also overload facilities by getting people to demand more services than the system can handle, thus disorganizing and shutting it down.
- Distribute educational materials. For instance, you can send CDs and DVDs of talks and lectures to libraries.

Civil Disobedience

Non-cooperation is the refusal to cooperate with practices and policies that one believes to be unethical. When non-cooperation involves breaking the law, it is called civil disobedience. Activists should never participate in civil disobedience without proper training and they should never pressure others into joining them; civil disobedience requires a readiness and commitment that only comes from freely choosing to join the action.

When planning to engage in civil disobedience, you should prepare ahead of time by attending a civil disobedience training, learning about your rights and the tactics of intimidation used by law enforcement officials, and dressing as conservatively as possible so as not to be perceived as a "terrorist." If you will be staging a sit-in, your group should also prepare to remain in place to avoid triggering a violent response from police officers. Finally, you should have an *affinity group*. An affinity group is a small group of activists within the larger group, with whom you carry out acts of civil disobedience. These groups provide activists with support and preparation; for instance, members decide upon a designated legal advocate who won't get arrested and can support the others from the outside, and they plan who will get arrested first to protect those in the group who are more vulnerable to police violence, such as people of color.

Two of the most common acts of civil disobedience are invading and blocking the space of the opponent, and destroying property. Examples of the former include staging sit-ins, where activists use their bodies to block the opponent from entering or exiting a building, and entering a facility and taking possession of documents or animals, as with *open rescues*. In an open rescue, activists take the animals from a facility and bring them to an undisclosed sanctuary. They videotape the facility and the rescue, to publicize the conditions in which the animals have been kept and their commitment to the cause. They show themselves as willing to risk arrest because they fully believe in the rightness of their actions. Even when animals are not taken,

incriminating video footage that is obtained can have a significant impact, as was the case with the photos Alex Pacheco took
of the Silver Spring monkeys that led to a major public debate
about animal rights.

Property Destruction

Property destruction is a risky tactic. If it isn't well thought out
and executed it can alienate the public. It is not strategic to
destroy property when it is solely done to damage assets and cost
the opponent time and money, to send a message to the opponent and the public that the movement is serious, or to save
lives. These are short-term gains that come at a much greater
cost in the long term. Lakey says that, because the opposition has
a virtually unlimited capacity to rebuild itself, property destruction has almost no physical impact on the system, and its value
is therefore only *symbolic*.

Lakey maintains that property destruction has value as a symbolic act when the destroyed material represents something
already hated by the public. When activists destroy something
that is widely reviled, such as a dictator's statue, the act represents
courage and determination and the activists are seen as heroes.
But when the material is not something the majority hates, it is
the *character* of the act—destruction—that the public focuses on,
and the activists are seen as terrorists. For example, when activists
set fire to research laboratories, facilities that to much of the public are centers for lifesaving scientific advancements, it is the
destruction—the violence—that gets highlighted. Activists are
portrayed as dangerous, criminal, and anti-human. And when tax-
payers have subsidized the property, the public is further angered.
Even when a company is not state-subsidized, owners can argue

that the destruction will drive up the cost of their products, with the burden falling on the consumer.

Property destruction is only strategic when it supports the broader strategy of the movement: attracting supporters. The way to use it for animal liberation is to either destroy your *own* property, such as throwing animal-tested cosmetics you purchased into a bonfire; destroy small amounts of *discarded* property, like an old gestation crate or instruments used to castrate unanaesthetized calves; or destroy *symbolic* property—mock pieces of property—such as dumping biodegradable mock dollar bills over the side of a boat in a reenactment of the Boston Tea Party, to demonstrate how taxes are wasted on agricultural subsidies. In each case, you have to be explicit that the property you're destroying was neither stolen nor costly to the public.

Working with the Media

The media are the primary outlet for reaching the public. You need to understand how to use the media strategically, so that your message is as accurately and widely conveyed as possible. Otherwise, not only will you receive no (or inaccurate) coverage; your opponents will ensure that it is *their* side of the issue that gets publicized. Therefore, you should frame tactics so that, if you do attract the press, your message will be heard the way you want it to.

Many activists are understandably skeptical of mainstream media corporations. However, these institutions are comprised of individuals who may have interests that differ from those of their employer. It is important that you establish positive, professional, and ongoing relationships with reporters and journalists, particularly those who have demonstrated an interest in issues involving animals. (For resources on how to most effectively work with the media, see www.lanternbooks.com/media.) Following are general guidelines:

- Do your research. Read up on how to most effectively work with the media.
- Entertainment sells. Keep your tactics interesting.
- Call a press conference to publicize the issue.
- Be clear about who your audience is and what they need to see and hear to support your campaign.
- Try to get media coverage when you kick off your campaign.
- Think in snapshots, and frame your tactics accordingly.
- Get quotes from experts, especially those who have switched sides.[18]
- Use images and symbols that Americans can relate to, such as staging a reenactment of the Boston Tea Party.
- Have visible signs of your organization's name, your sound bite, and your Web site everywhere and, whenever possible, mention the name of your organization and its demand, succinctly. For example, "United for Animals is here today to demand the immediate termination of Brigg University's burned dog experiments."[19]
- Issue a press release.
- Use local media venues, as they are often looking for new issues.
- Alert all media in the area of your upcoming event.
- Frame your message in a sound bite—a brief, powerful, and quotable line—that is repeated throughout the campaign and used by everyone who is interviewed.

- Never trust a statement as being "off the record," even if this is what you are told.

- Try to have people tell their personal stories to the media, of why they joined the campaign and how the issue has affected them.

- Have spokespersons who are designated interviewees and have prepared comments.

- Have a "news center" or "media room" link on your Web site, which contains information for interested media correspondents and information about past media events.[20]

- If the media misrepresents your event, make this public. You can approach another media corporation to expose the one that misrepresented you.

- Try not to directly threaten the interests of the media or its current sponsors.

- Don't get defensive or let the media deflect attention from the issue, and don't feel you have to answer all questions, especially hypothetical ones.[21]

As Henry Spira demonstrated, a strategic campaign for animals can have a major and lasting impact on the movement as a whole. Campaigns are like the DNA of the movement. When dysfunctional, they can kill it. But when healthy, they keep it alive and thriving.

6

⁂

Power to the People—and Animals
Starting a Grassroots Organization for Animals

> *Never doubt that a small group of thoughtful, committed citizens can change the world. Indeed, it is the only thing that ever has.* —Margaret Mead

FOR ANY NUMBER of reasons, you may want to start your own organization for animals. Starting a new organization can be an exciting undertaking and can enable you to have a significant impact on the lives of animals and activists alike.

However, starting an organization for animals can also lead to the demise of energetic, motivated, and skilled activists; animal liberation groups form and dissolve all the time. All too often, activists who are either disenchanted with their current organization or are without an organization and are hungry for a vehicle through which to channel their energy for animals start their own group without having fully prepared for such a monumental task. They end up frustrated and exhausted. Like everything else, starting your own organization for animals must be strategic in order to be successful.

A strategic grassroots organization for animals must be *needed* and *feasible*. Before you make the decision to start your own organization, you should answer the following questions:

- What issue will be the focus of your organization? Vivisection? Meat? Circuses?
- Do you want to start a local chapter (division) of a national organization instead of founding your own organization? If you choose to start a chapter of a national organization, you may get support—such as funding, structure, and staff—but you will have to accept the ideology and policies of the parent organization.
- Is there a need for this kind of organization? For example, if you are starting an anti-fur group, are there already groups in your area working on this issue?
- Is your area appropriate for the kind of organization you want to start? For instance, if you plan to fight certain types of companies, are there local companies you can effectively target? Are the residents likely to be supportive of the issue?
- Do you have the resources to start your own organization? How much time, energy, and money can you realistically invest?

If you conclude that there is a need for a new organization for animals in your area, and you have the means with which to start one, you need to consider one final, but most important

question: *Are you willing to commit to the project for the long haul?*
Starting an organization is exhilarating, and it's natural to begin
with boundless energy and optimism. Activists often assume that
this enthusiasm will never abate and, when it inevitably does,
they become discouraged and lose motivation.

Starting your own organization is like starting a personal relationship. In the beginning, it's romantic and you are full of passion
and hope. Yet, as with any relationship, the honeymoon period
ends and reality sets in. Your phone calls to promising supporters
are never returned. The copy machine is irreparably quirky and
the furniture that was donated from the company down the street
smells bad. The treasurer has a sick child and hasn't been in contact with the group for over a week. The organizational development books you ordered were sent to the wrong address. Jonas
and Sara seem unable to agree on anything. And so on. The reality of starting your own organization is much less glamorous than
the dream; the work is often tedious and frustrating. However, if
you are prepared for this eventuality and are committed to the
long haul, you can create a strategic grassroots organization that
has the potential to make the world a better place for animals.

What Is a Grassroots Organization for Animals?

Grassroots organizing is based on a bottom-up power model,
hence its name. The roots of grass sustain and nourish the blades,
enabling the grass to grow. The power of a grassroots organization comes from those in the community in which it's based. It
is organized by and for the same people. Therefore, grassroots
organizations are always local. And it is these local organizations
that form the power base of the movement—the larger national and international organizations depend on the support of

local groups, though the grassroots organizations are, as their name suggests, hidden below the surface.

Because grassroots organizations are typically comprised of those whose interests they serve, they are less likely to get side-tracked from their agenda. Technically, everyone in the organization is invested in fulfilling its mission for his or her own benefit. However, animal liberation organizations lack the voices of those they've been established to protect, and so it's important for organizers not to allow their own agenda to override that of the organization.

Getting Started

Before launching your organization, you need to lay the groundwork. The first step is to do your research, learning as much as you can about the process of starting a grassroots organization. There are some excellent books on this subject; see www.lanternbooks.com/readings for a list of the ones I recommend.

To get started, you will need to choose your organizational model, determine who your core staff will be, develop mission and values statements, create a budget and funding plan, and develop a long-term strategic plan.

Organizational and Financial Models

It's important to be clear about your organizational model right from the start, since your model will guide your mission and practices. You will need to decide whether your model will be *advocacy*, *educational*, *direct service*, *direct action*, or some combination of these. I described these models in Chapter 4, so you may want to refer back to that chapter.

Also, though you may not know what kind of financial model you will ultimately use until your organization has developed, you should start considering this issue. Your financial model determines what kind of funding you can receive and what your legal status will be. You have several choices as to what kind of financial model you adopt. What you decide will depend on the size of your group and the nature of your work. You can choose whether to incorporate and whether to seek nonprofit status (and what type of nonprofit status to adopt). The laws governing these issues are complex, and you should discuss your options with an attorney before taking any formal action. Following is a brief explanation of each financial model.

Incorporation

To *incorporate* is to legally form a corporation. Incorporation does *not* equate to profit; many nonprofit organizations are incorporated. The reason organizations incorporate is to protect their staff from liability. If you are incorporated and, for example, your organization goes into debt or gets sued, your staff's assets, such as their retirement plans, have some protection. In such a case, the assets at risk are generally those of the organization itself. The assets of your staff become at risk if your organization dissolves because of *internal corruption*, such as illegal acts committed by your officers or Board members. The Midwest Academy says that incorporation also helps to protect you against "slap suits," which are lawsuits filed by the opposition during a campaign, in order to frighten and distract organizers from their work.

The laws for incorporation vary from state to state. If you

are interested in incorporating, you should refer to the Web site for your state's Secretary of State's Office or, as it is called in some states, Department of State.

NonProfit Organizations

Non-profit (sometimes referred to as not-for-profit) organizations exist to serve a purpose beyond garnering profits for themselves. Nonprofit organizations can, and do, make a profit. They simply don't give the profit to individual members, with the exception of paying salaries; all surplus funds must go back into the organization itself. You would file for nonprofit status if you wanted your organization to be exempt from paying federal income taxes and to be able to accept tax-deductible donations.

There are different types of nonprofit organizations, each with different types of restrictions and benefits. Once an organization is granted nonprofit status, it is restricted in its ability to perform certain activities. For instance, an organization the mission of which is to ban dog racing may not be permitted to carry out certain election-related and lobbying actions. Activists sometimes create more than one organization, each with a different legal status, to receive the maximum financial benefit without having to adhere to as many restrictions. Following are the types of nonprofit organizations you could consider applying for.

501(c)(3) Organizations

The most common type of nonprofit organization has 501(c)(3) status. These organizations receive the greatest tax benefits but also have the most restrictions. The activities of 501(c)(3) organizations are limited to those that are educational, scientific, or charitable. For instance, 501(c)(3) organizations can engage in non-partisan voter education activities, such as educating the public about dog racing, but they cannot endorse or oppose any candidate who's running for office.

501(c)(4) Organizations

501(c)(4) organizations are called "social welfare organizations" or "civic leagues." They have fewer restrictions than do 501(c)(3) organizations, giving activists more freedom to lobby and advocate. The drawback is that 501(c)(4) organizations receive fewer tax benefits; though organizers don't have to pay most federal taxes, donations are not tax deductible.

527 Organizations

527 organizations are called "political action committees" or "PACs," and they exist to either support or oppose candidates for public office. Political parties and campaigns are examples of some 527 organizations.

Combining Organizations

A variety of combinations are possible when you want to create, or work with, other organizations to maximize your efforts. One common method is for organizers in a larger 501(c)(3) organization to start up a 501(c)(4) organization—or a grassroots organization that doesn't apply for nonprofit status—that is funded by the mother organization. Or organizers in a 501(c)(4) organization may create a 501(c)(3) organization in order to receive more funds. Either or both of these groups may start up a 527 organization to enable them to lobby for animal-friendly public officials.

If you are interested in applying for nonprofit status, there's an excellent publication from The Alliance for Justice that you should review: *The Connection: Strategies for Creating and Operating 501(c)(3)s, 501(c)(4)s, and PACs*. In addition, the IRS publishes a booklet, which is available online as well, called *Tax Exempt Status for Your Organization* ("Publication 557"). This is an excellent resource for starting up a nonprofit organization.

Choosing Core Staff

To start up your organization, you need to decide who your core staff will be: How many of you are committed to meeting and working regularly, and what will your roles and responsibilities be? Do you need to recruit other volunteers for startup, or does your core group possess the necessary skills for this purpose? Your core group should either have or be willing to learn leadership, fundraising, and administrative skills. As your organization grows you can bring in staff to fill new roles as the need for them emerges.

Developing Your Mission Statement

Your mission statement defines the purpose and goals of your organization, and it should be drafted and agreed upon by all core staff. As I mentioned in Chapter 4, your mission statement outlines the purpose of your organization. It answers the question *Why does the organization exist?* How you answer this question will depend in part on what your organizational model is. The sample mission statement I used in Chapter 4 was from the New England Anti-Vivisection Society (NEAVS), and it included the goal "to expose and replace animal experiments ... with ... modern research methods."

Mission statements vary in length from a few sentences to over a page. It's best, however, to keep the statement as concise as possible; otherwise, it risks becoming confusing or overly ambitious. Following are some questions to help you draft your mission statement:

- Who will benefit from the organization?
- What will these benefits be?
- How do we want others to view the organization?
- What are the values that will guide the organization?

You should revisit your mission statement regularly, to ensure that you are staying on track with your goals.

Developing Your Values Statement

Your values statement reflects the core values of your organization. These include the values of your mission and of your organization's culture. The values of your organizational culture determine how your organization and its members operate on a daily basis. For example, if one of your values is to cultivate diversity, you would make sure to recruit staff and members from diverse backgrounds and to respect different opinions as they emerge.

Your values statement should include approximately four to six core values, one of which should be a commitment to practicing cooperative power, which will inform the actions of your group. These values should be clear, realistic, and understood by everybody. Far too often, organizers draft values statements that they pay lip service to but never follow, or they archive their values statement and forget about it. Be careful to avoid falling into this trap. Hang your values statement in a place where it is visible to everybody in the organization, and make sure new staff members understand it. If you can stay on track with your values, your organization is much more likely to follow its mission and be healthy, powerful, and strategic.

Developing a Budget

Developing a comprehensive budget is complex, so as your organization grows you should continue learning about this process. (For resources on developing a budget, see www. lanternbooks.com/budget.)

In the beginning, you need to determine how much money you need in order to start up. What are your immediate expenses? For instance, do you need to pay for postage and mailing materials? Photocopies? Utilities? Phone bills? Travel expenses, including gas and tolls? Campaign materials, such as posterboard, banners, and costumes? Project how much these items will cost over a year's time, and with your core group, create a budget that includes these expenses. You should try to get as many items as possible donated. For example, you could ask to use meeting space in your local YMCA or community center, and you might be able to get office equipment donated from local companies. Your basic annual expenses will probably include rent, utilities, training (e.g., books on organizing), salaries, consultants (if you decide to file for nonprofit status you will need a lawyer and you may want an accountant to help with start up), travel expenses, office equipment (computers, paper, copiers, phones, etc.), and fundraising activities, which are discussed in the following section. Whenever you run a campaign, you will need to include the campaign as an expense in your organizational budget and then develop a sub-budget specifically for that campaign.

During start up, you can get by with just covering expenses. However, if you want your organization to grow, you will need to start bringing in more money than you spend. This requires a funding plan.

Developing a Funding Plan

Your funding plan is part of your budget. Like your budget, your funding plan should be modified as your organization grows. For start up, however, you will only need to determine how to cover your immediate and first-year expenses.

Make a list of all sources of income you expect to generate, including non-monetary sources, such as donated office equipment. Will you apply for government grants? Funding from a national animal liberation organization? Will you solicit corporate donors? Individual contributors? How you obtain funding will help you decide whether to file for nonprofit status. You don't have to have all of this figured out right away, but you should put together a draft of your funding plan to guide you during your startup phase.

As time goes on, you'll need to become adept at fundraising. An excellent resource is *The Grassroots Fundraising Book*, by Joan Flanagan. Following are some of Flanagan's principles of grassroots fundraising:

- All fundraising efforts should serve three purposes: to raise money, to heighten awareness about your organization and campaign, and to help people feel engaged and empowered.
- Use every fundraising event as an opportunity to promote your organization and campaign.
- Learn all you can about fundraising. You can start by deter-

mining what information your group members already have and then brainstorm together. You can also learn what other organizations have done and determine why their efforts have or haven't been successful.

- Create a one-year strategic plan specifically for fundraising. Eventually, create a five-year plan. If possible, have a fundraising committee to work on these plans.

- Create a strategic plan for each fundraising effort.

- Keep good records of your events (amount of money spent and raised, contacts, vendors, donors, etc.) and a file of ideas as they are generated.

- Budget money and time specifically for fundraising.

- Recognize everyone who gives, no matter how small the contribution. Send everyone a thank-you note and make major donors visible by naming them either verbally or in writing.

- Use press releases, radio and television public service announcements, free classifieds, fliers, posters, and other organizations' newsletters to publicize your event.

Flanagan also suggests the following fundraising activities:

- Organize food tastings in which you charge admission to attendees. You can have vegetarian-friendly restaurants and whole food stores donate food to promote their businesses.

- Hold phone-a-thons, ideally with donated phones.

- Solicit donations from businesses that support your purpose, such as whole foods grocers or animal-friendly retailers like The Body Shop. This can help companies improve their public image and promote themselves.

- Go door-to-door canvassing.
- Send out direct mailings to residents of your community whom you think would support your cause.
- Publish a newsletter.
- Hold a special event, such as a rummage sale with donated goods; a holiday fundraiser, such as a Halloween haunted house; a raffle; or an auction with donated items.

Understanding Administration

Many eager and motivated activists start an organization, only to find after a short time that they've neglected the most important part of their work: administrative duties. Administrative duties are not as glamorous or interesting as what many activists consider the "real" work of organizing. However, an organization is an administrative body and if you don't take care of its body, it will die. The mundane tasks of running an organization are the foundation that enables it to carry out its mission. These tasks include the day-to-day responsibilities of maintaining your organization, as well as the organization's staffing patterns and policies. As with other aspects of start up, you should do some research to better familiarize yourself with the issue.

With your core group, decide what tasks need to be done daily, weekly, monthly, and quarterly, and who will be responsible for different tasks. Who will monitor phone calls? Keep track of volunteers? Coordinate meetings? Keep track of donations? Monitor expenditures? Manage files?

The Midwest Academy says that central to controlling your administrative systems is developing a well-organized filing system, remembering that the purpose of files is to *retrieve* information, not tuck it away. The Midwest Academy suggests that one way to keep your files organized is to keep separate files for each campaign. These files can include, for example, newspaper clippings, all correspondence, research data on your targets, and campaign strategies. You should review and clean out your files regularly.

Staffing Your Organization

Even if your organization starts out with just a small group of core activists, you should draft a written personnel policy. Your personnel policy states your organization's policies regarding staff, and it should reflect your values statement. As your group grows, you can make your personnel policy more comprehensive.

For start up, your policy should cover *work schedules*, including how many hours people are expected to work, how to manage time off for emergencies, vacations, or holidays, and what to do when the weather is severe; *hiring or recruitment*, including a statement of non-discrimination on the basis of gender, ethnicity, sexual orientation, etc.; *assessment of organizers' performance*, including how and when assessment will occur; *how you will handle conflict*; *firing*, or what constitutes grounds for dismissal; *reimbursement for expenses*; and *special office requirements*, such as requiring that the office be vegan. Everyone in your group needs to be clear and in agreement about what is expected of them and each other. Your personnel policy will help people stay on track, manage conflict responsibly, and avoid the infighting that is often caused by people having different, unspoken expectations.

As with your mission and values statements, your personnel policy must be agreed upon by everyone in your core group. You should review other organizations' personnel policies when drafting your own—there are plenty of samples in books and online—and adapt them for your group.

Hierarchy and Supervision

Many activists are opposed to hierarchy and attempt to structure their organizations accordingly. However, hierarchy isn't an all-or-nothing concept. It exists as a matter of degree. Virtually all organizations will have some degree of hierarchy, since this is the most familiar and often most effective way to run an organization. When your group starts out it may be more egalitarian, as there are few organizers and responsibility is evenly distributed. However, as soon as you start to recruit volunteers and fill staffing positions you will likely have established a hierarchical order. How well you deal with this depends on how well you are able to supervise (and perhaps be supervised by) others. It's not whether you have a hierarchy, but how you relate to it that matters.

In all types of organizations, from grassroots startups to for-profit corporations, people find themselves in supervisory roles having received little or no training in how to manage people. One of the primary reasons organizations founder is inadequate supervision. Dedicated activists who are thrilled to be given an opportunity to actually get paid for their work can quickly find themselves resentful and disillusioned when their supervisor is ineffective, and quit the organization. And for those who are volunteers, it is even easier to walk away. High turnover rates are a serious problem for many animal liberation organizations. However, with proper guidance you can learn effective supervision.

The principles of leadership, advocacy, communication, and

facilitation discussed throughout this book also apply to being an effective supervisor. On top of these, effective supervisors are skilled at problem solving, decision making, delegation, hiring and training new recruits, goal setting, offering constructive feedback, and ensuring that the organizational values are respected. You can learn supervisory skills from reading books, attending workshops, or getting mentoring from seasoned supervisors.

Avoiding Founder's Syndrome

Founder's Syndrome is a problem that can occur when a founder, founders, or any leaders of an organization have too much power over the decision-making process. The organization takes on the personality of these individuals and everyone else is dependent on them for guidance. This makes the organization unbalanced and unsustainable: when the key leaders leave the organization, there is no one left to carry on the work.

To avoid Founder's Syndrome, the organization must be independent of those who control it. It has to be an entity in its own right, rather than just a project that belongs to an individual or a small group. Pay close attention to whether the Board and other members of the organization are looking to one person or a select group for guidance, and if so, intervene by allocating responsibility more democratically. If members seem resistant to accepting more responsibility, you should have a meeting to address their concerns. You can also write into policy a "succession plan," which is a plan to determine the course of action should the leaders resign.

Starting your own organization for animals can be an empowering and rewarding experience. The animal liberation movement has evolved largely because of activists who have created strategic grassroots organizations. The power of the movement resides in the people, working together, from the roots up.

7

＊

Power Parasites
The Silent Killers of Organizations

When the power of love overcomes the love of power the world will know peace.—Jimi Hendrix

We thought, because we had power, we had wisdom.
—Stephen Vincent Benét

YOU CAN FOLLOW all the basic protocol for developing a strategic organization and still end up unsuccessful. This is because there are silent killers that attack an organization from within and remain invisible until—and often even after—the organization has disintegrated. These killers are not individuals; they are dysfunctional power dynamics that are so insidious they are arguably the leading cause of death among animal liberation organizations. I refer to them as *power parasites*, forces that prey upon their host, consuming it from the inside until they eventually kill it.

There are two strains of power parasites, which are actually two sides of the same coin: *addictive* and *traumatic* power dynamics. Both are progressive, in that the longer they exist, the more entrenched and destructive they become. In other words, they grow stronger with use. These dynamics will eventually lead to the death of your organization, so recognizing them is essential for a strategic organization for animals.

Part I: Addictive Organizational Dynamics

An addict is a person who is dependent on either a *substance*, such as drugs or alcohol, or a *process*, such as gambling, activism, or helping others. Most addicts are not aware that they have an addiction, and see their behavior as normal. In fact, addicts are masters at rationalizing their behavior, saying they can quit whenever they want, pointing out that others are doing the same thing, and justifying why it's necessary that they continue doing what they've been doing. However, all addicts are in fact stuck in self-destructive patterns of behavior that, on some level, they feel powerless to change. These patterns of behavior, if not broken, can lead the addict to "bottom out" or, in activist terminology, burn out. And burnout is contagious—so when one person suffers from it, others can start to feel the effects as well, leading to the breakdown of the organizational system.

Addictive Organizations

Organizations are *systems*, in that they are *entities comprised of two or more individuals*. Regardless of their size, all systems—from couples to an entire movement—are greater than the sum of their parts. The system has its own character, or personality. If your organization has twenty staff members, the combination of all of their personalities creates the personality of the organization.

Although systems are shaped by the individuals that comprise them, they also shape those same individuals. For example, if your organization contains a number of activists that overwork, then a newly hired staff member will be expected to overwork as well, even if this is not his or her normal behavior. Parasitic organizations force people to conform to unhealthy behaviors, and they resist any challenge to their status quo. They maintain themselves by rewarding people for conformity and punishing people for deviating from established practices. The very structure of the organization is set up to create and maintain a dysfunctional way of relating to power.

One type of parasitic organization is the *addictive organization*. In their groundbreaking book *The Addictive Organization*, organizational consultants Anne Wilson Schaef and Diane Fassel argue that, like individuals, systems can be addicts. These *addictive systems* share the same characteristics as individual addicts except that the addictive behaviors get expressed *between* (or among) individuals, in their interpersonal dynamics and in the processes of the system. Since an organization is a system, organizations can be addictive systems; they are addictive organizations. While an organization can become addictive because one or more of its top executives are addicts and set the tone for everyone else, more often the problem is embedded within the structure of the organization itself. The organization is set up to cultivate and maintain addictive behaviors that are expressed through, for example, interpersonal conflicts, disorganized meetings, elitism and secrecy, unclear or unrealistic job descriptions, mixed messages, indirect communications, and workaholism.

In Chapter 4, I pointed out that the structure of an organization has to be congruent with its mission, or its purpose. In a healthy organization, the structure is the framework that enables the organization to fulfill its mission. In an addictive organization, Wilson Schaef and Fassel argue, the structure and mission have become incongruent. Often, activists join an organization because they believe in its mission, but find themselves working toward very different goals. Rather than develop campaigns or raise money for animals in need, their efforts may go toward furthering an organizational executive's career or to simply putting out fires. Activists may end up supporting something that is totally different from, and even contradictory to, the reason they originally joined the organization. Wilson Schaef and Fassel say that the structure of the addictive organization is also rigid and punitive. Employees are treated as though they aren't trustworthy, and are sometimes harshly punished for not following even petty rules. Activists become demoralized and resentful, and therefore may act out the very behaviors the organization is supposedly controlling for.

Hidden Addictions

Addictive systems are difficult to recognize for a number of reasons. One reason is because addictive behaviors are so common as to be unremarkable, so they go unnoticed in most organizations. It seems perfectly normal, for instance, that staff members work overtime without compensation, clash with one another around trivial issues, complain when people leave meetings that are running overtime, take on more work than they can comfortably handle, act out their personal issues on others, and insist that everything's fine when they're under unmanageable stress.

And if you have a personal history of addiction, whereby a loved one or yourself has been an addict, you could be so accustomed to addictive behaviors that they're almost impossible to detect.

According to Wilson Schaef and Fassel, another reason addictive systems are so difficult to recognize is that they employ defense mechanisms to mask the addictive behaviors. As with individual addicts, *denial* is their primary method of defense. A person can be in the throes of a full-blown addiction that is glaringly obvious to everyone around and still insist that nothing's wrong. An addictive organization can be replete with crises, conflicts, and chaos, and staff will blame certain individuals for the problems rather than admit that the system is sick. "Problem" staff members leave the organization, only to be replaced by people who end up having the very same issues. Other defense mechanisms addictive systems use include *justification* ("The 'squeaky wheel' was let go because she just wasn't a team player."); *avoidance* ("We'll discuss your concern about having too heavy a workload after this campaign is over. But for now, we need your full commitment."); and *dissociation* ("I know the organization has a lot of problems, but they really don't affect me. I just do my own thing and don't get involved in the politics.").

Addictive systems are also difficult to identify because the individuals within them may not *want* to identify them. Admitting to the problem would mean that they would have to make changes in their own lives in order to break their familiar patterns of behavior. That which is familiar, even if it's uncomfortable, is safe, and so familiarity is often preferable to change. For example, activists may complain endlessly about not having enough support for a campaign, but when new staff are hired for this purpose, the original activists may feel that they've lost their control over the project, resent the new hires, and drive them to resign by not giving them proper guidance.

Characteristics of Addictive Organizations

Wilson Schaef and Fassel argue that certain characteristics are hallmarks of the addictive organization. These characteristics exist to keep the system intact. They include: *confusion or lack of clarity* whereby, for instance, skilled executives have meetings in which they endlessly brainstorm without any clear outcome;[22] *perfectionism*, which creates undue pressure and an atmosphere of anxiety; and *negativism*. Other characteristics are *forgetfulness* ("I meant to start calling applicants so you don't have to keep doing this job alone, but it just slipped my mind—again."); *dependency* ("My hands are tied until John gets me that report"); and *fear*— of losing one's job, being gossiped about, failure, etc. Additionally, addictions expert Jean Kinney describes addictive systems as being *crisis oriented*, *secretive*, and *chaotic*. And in *Addictive Thinking*, psychiatrist Abraham Twerski says that addicts tend toward *self-deception*, *projection* (blaming others for their feelings and problems) *hypersensitivity*, *manipulation*, and *irrationality*. Other characteristics of the addictive system that Wilson Schaef and Fassel have observed are explored below.

The Scarcity Model

The scarcity model is a way of viewing the world in which important resources, including time and energy, seem scarce. The scarcity model is usually a given among activists. You may feel that, no matter what you do, you never have enough time or energy for your efforts to make a significant difference for animals. This is in part because there is truth that your efforts *are* never enough—to bring about animal liberation anytime soon. However, your efforts are often more than enough to work toward the goals of your organization, which is realistically all that matters. The addictive organization tends to minimize staff members' accomplishments and pressure them to overwork, thereby promoting the scarcity model. Activists who started out feeling empowered and energized end up frustrated, despairing, and burning out.

The Illusion of Control

Addicts are out of control—of their addiction, and often of themselves. So, too, are addictive systems. Staff members can feel powerless, so they *pretend* to be in control ("I can quit whenever I want") and may attempt to control others—other staff, projects, decisions, and many other elements of the organization. Addictive organizations encourage controlling behaviors, as when executives are expected to micromanage their staff.

Frozen Feelings

Addictions serve to block and numb, or "freeze" unpleasant feelings. Addictive systems both numb the feelings of individuals within the system and prevent these individuals from expressing authentic emotions. Staff may be understandably angry, afraid, or depressed, but they are not allowed to express this. So, they engage in increasingly addictive behavior in an attempt to stuff their feelings back down. You may, for instance, find yourself feeling anxious about launching an important new campaign. If your organization is addictive, you might be discouraged from sharing your fear and expected to act "as if"—as if you're much more self-assured than you actually feel. You may pour yourself more fully into your work to distract yourself from your anxiety and give yourself a false sense of confidence.

The Promise

No doubt you were drawn to your organization because of its promise. The promise is embedded in the mission of the organization: it is the promise of what the organization will accomplish if people just keep working at it. In a healthy organization, staff members feel empowered, as they genuinely work toward the goal of fulfilling the promise. But in an addictive organization, the promise exists in theory only. It is the carrot that dangles in front of the disillusioned activist, keeping him or her hooked to the organization. Another kind of promise is the promise that things will get better when, for instance, the current crisis or campaign ends or the director is replaced. Activists often remain in dysfunctional organizations because, as with other dysfunctional relationships, they believe that if they just try hard enough or wait long enough, the honeymoon phase will return.

Invalidation

Invalidation is the discounting of any ideas or experiences that don't support the system. Invalidation may take the form of a "personality conflict." For example, you and your supervisor might be in conflict over his or her continual refusal to approve vacation time you've requested. Your supervisor might evade your requests, and invalidate your need for time off, by constantly telling you it's "not a good time." And other staff might further invalidate you by dismissing the conflict as an interpersonal issue, a clash of personalities, instead of recognizing it as an addictive dynamic.

Dualism

Dualism is either/or thinking. Organizational dualisms cast ideas and experiences as opposites, often in conflict with one another. People are seen as good or bad, right or wrong. In the addictive organization, dualism can take the form of, "If you aren't for the action, you're against it," and "Either you commit to working on the whole project, or don't bother working on it at all." Also, people are judged based on their behavior; if someone does something "bad" they are seen as a "bad" person.

Ethical Deterioration

The obvious end result of engaging in addictive dynamics is the deterioration of one's ethics. Controlling others, being dishonest about one's feelings, and invalidating the truth are behaviors that erode one's sense of personal integrity. The ethical deterioration of the system progresses until abuse becomes the norm, making many activists' actions seem little different from those of the people and organizations they are fighting.

Activism as an Addiction

Few things are nobler than working to make the world a better place. Some of the most admirable people in history have dedicated their lives to alleviating suffering and fighting injustice. However, there is a fine line between dedication and addiction. Dedication is healthy and productive; addiction is unhealthy and ultimately destructive. Animal liberation activism is naturally addictive. Because animal exploitation is so extensive and the emotions it evokes so powerful, it is all too easy to become consumed with working harder in an attempt to alleviate both animal suffering and the painful feelings it evokes.

Addiction to activism is a kind of workaholism. Workaholism isn't simply working hard; it is working in order to avoid uncomfortable feelings or issues. If you are a workaholic, you probably become anxious or depressed when you have downtime. Work has become your sole focus; it takes precedence over other aspects of life, including family, friends, and even self-care. The addicted activist needs activism in order to feel like a worthy person, and sometimes in order to feel at all, as life without activism can seem dull and meaningless. Workaholics often have other addictions, as well. Psychologist Robert Pasick points out that people typically mask the effects of overworking by using stimulants to stay awake and alcohol or other depressants to help them unwind from the stress of their work.

The addictive organization encourages workaholism, expecting staff to be single-mindedly dedicated to the cause and loyal to the organization to the point where it is assumed they will participate in organizational activities outside of working hours and the workplace. Wilson Schaef and Fassel say that, even when addictive organizations appear to discourage workaholism by, for instance, offering stress-reduction workshops, their actual practices don't reflect a concern for employee welfare. For instance, a staff member once told me that when he left work at the end of a ten-hour day, his supervisor off handedly commented, "Too bad meatpackers don't stop working at seven p.m., too."

The addicted activist doesn't necessarily need to be encouraged or manipulated into "giving their all" to the organization. As Wilson Schaef and Fassel point out, organizations often fulfill needs that people didn't get from their families of origin: a sense of belonging and purpose, the ability to have influence and control, and recognition and caring. Organizations can also give people a sense of power—the power to heal/save others (as some activists may not have been able to do in their own families), and a chance to feel powerful as they challenge power in society. Activists who seek to get their basic needs met by their work often do so because they experience some degree of *codependency*.

Codependency

Codependency is a particular kind of dynamic. *Codependents* are loosely defined as people who are addicted to helping others, and they are naturally drawn toward victims. Wilson Schaef and Fassel say that, as with individual codependents, who are the classic "enablers" of alcoholics, codependents in an organization enable the addictive system.

Codependents are caretakers. They often grew up in households where they had to take on the role of parent, either caring for their own parents, siblings, or both. Or, their parents simply didn't provide them with adequate parenting. As children, codependents often couldn't say no, either because they felt too guilty and/or because they weren't permitted to go against the wishes of their parents. They have learned to take on more responsibility than they feel comfortable with to avoid letting others down and because they feel more secure knowing that others depend on them. Essentially, codependents *need* to be *needed*. People are often attracted to activism because they grew up believing that it was their responsibility to take care of others. So, it's not surprising that activist organizations have a high percentage of codependents.

Codependency expert Pia Mellody describes five core characteristics of codependents: they have *inadequate levels of self-esteem*; they have *difficulty defining their own reality*; they have *diffi-*

culty identifying and managing their needs; they have *difficulty setting appropriate boundaries*; and they exhibit *extreme behaviors*. Each of these characteristics is expressed in behaviors that feed the addictive organization and are explained below.

Inadequate Levels of Self-Esteem

If you have healthy self-esteem, you feel that you are inherently worthy, equal to others, regardless of the circumstances. You feel empowered. Because codependents learned that they are more or less worthy based on what they do rather than who they are, they can flip between feeling "less-than" (worthless and inferior) and "better than" (grandiose and superior). How powerful they feel is determined by how well they perform and how others regard them.

In activist organizations, codependents may directly or indirectly denigrate others in order to boost their own sense of worth and compete to win the favor of those in positions of power. And because their self-esteem is based on how others regard them, they often avoid conflict for fear of being disliked. They may therefore act out *passive-aggressively*. Passive-aggressive behavior is an indirect way of expressing anger. For example, an activist who feels unappreciated by his supervisor may start "forgetting" to follow through on tasks. Avoiding conflict can also lead to sending mixed messages. People who fear upsetting others may agree to something they don't want and then not keep their promises.

Difficulty Managing One's Own Reality

Codependents were taught to distrust their own experience. For example, a parent may tell a boy who's crying because he fell down and skinned his knee to stop being so "dramatic" and that if he doesn't stop crying, he'll "really get something to cry about." The boy learns to believe that others know his experience better than he does.

When the boy has grown into a man, he may depend on others to tell him how he's feeling and believe them when they do. Or, he may be totally disconnected from his feelings and deny he even has any, even when people point out otherwise. Another possibility is that, if he *is* aware of his feelings, he may be reluctant to share them for fear of being told he's wrong. He may also reenact his father's behavior on others, telling his coworkers, for instance, that they're overreacting when they're upset about a failed project. He can also have difficulty making appropriate decisions since he isn't in touch with how he feels, and may cover up his mistakes for fear of being criticized and feeling like a "bad" employee. All of these issues can cause serious interpersonal problems within an organization.

Difficulty Identifying and Managing One's Needs

When someone either doesn't know what they need or doesn't feel comfortable asking for what they need, they attempt to get their needs met using indirect means. For instance, rather than say that she is feeling burned out from overworking and requesting time off, an activist may start showing up late to work, calling in sick, or not completing projects.

Difficulty Setting Functional Boundaries

Because their parents didn't respect their boundaries, codependents didn't learn how to set healthy boundaries for themselves. Parents can cross children's boundaries by, for instance, physically abusing them or invalidating their feelings, as with the example of the boy above. As adults, codependents often invade others' boundaries (acting out of a sense of entitlement), allow their own boundaries to be invaded, or both. For instance, a director may feel entitled to walk into others' offices uninvited or unannounced, micromanage, or call on staff outside of working hours. Or, an activist may not stand up to colleagues who try to control his work or treat him condescendingly.

Extreme Behaviors
Codependents tend to have trouble doing things in moderation, which can lead to perfectionism and excessive working and, because it's their norm, the expectation that others behave similarly. This can take the form of martyrdom, whereby they sacrifice themselves and judge others for not putting forth as much effort.

Codependents aren't "bad" people. They are people whose attitudes and behaviors are largely positive; caring for others and working to help them are admirable qualities. However, these qualities, when taken to the extreme and when stemming from a need for power, end up counterproductive. As with codependents, addictive organizations are not "bad" organizations. If you find that your organization is addictive, it's best to look at it simply as an infected system in need of healing.

Part II: Traumatic Organizational Dynamics
The traumatic organization is similar to the addictive organization, in that it is a self-destructive system in which power is

abused. Traumatic and addictive organizational dynamics overlap with and reinforce one another.

Traumatic organizations are comprised of people whose personal traumatization is unresolved. A trauma can be caused by obvious victimization, such as child abuse or rape, but it can result from more subtle forms of abuse as well, such as emotional neglect. People who aren't direct victims of violence can also become traumatized through witnessing violence, especially when they feel powerless to prevent it. And research has shown that two factors increase a person's risk for being traumatized by witnessing violence: having a high level of empathy, and having a personal trauma history. Both of these factors are common to animal liberation activists. Empathy enables people to care enough about animal suffering to feel compelled to alleviate it. Moreover, although people come into activism for a number of reasons, many of which are healthful and admirable, many activists are drawn to activism because of their own history of traumatization. If you feel called to animal liberation, you are probably able to identify with the sense of powerlessness and helplessness of the animals you seek to protect. One reason you may be able to feel such concern for the animals is because you, too, have known what it feels like to be on the receiving end of abuse of power. Animal liberation organizations are replete with traumatized activists.

The Trauma Triad

People who haven't resolved their personal traumas often re-create or act them out in what I refer to as the *trauma triad*. The trauma triad encompasses the three roles played in a traumatic event: victim, witness, and perpetrator. *Traumatic re-creations* in an organization are enactments of the trauma triad, when individuals or groups play one or more of these roles. I have seen these re-creations in every animal liberation organization I've worked with.

One story can illustrate this phenomenon. I worked as a volunteer for an animal liberation organization whose president was often referred to as a "fascist" and "loose cannon" by staff. The president favored a small group of executive elites (who retained their status by faithfully supporting all his actions) but was tyrannical toward everyone else, insulting and arbitrarily firing employees, sometimes a handful at a time. The organization had an employee turnover rate that rivaled that of McDonald's. Staff members were constantly on edge, wondering who would be berated or fired next and often competing with one another for membership in the president's club of favorites. The *perpetrators*—the president and his executive allies—would go on a rampage and fire a group of *victims*, while employee *witnesses* looked on from the sidelines. The perpetrator-victim-witness dynamic can play itself out in any number of ways, and people often switch roles, but in every case it is individually and organizationally destructive.

Part III. Treating the Parasitic Organization

Just as activism is ultimately about power, so, too, are addiction and trauma. Both of these parasites cause and are caused by disempowerment. Renowned traumatologist Judith Herman claims that the first principle of recovery is the empowerment of the survivor. In the case of the parasitic organization, "survivors" include individual activists and the organization itself. Therefore, while you must take responsibility for your own healing, you must also attend to the organizational dynamics that need to be reshaped.

All the elements of recovery are the opposite of those that comprise addictive and traumatic systems: honesty, openness, direct communication, authenticity, and integrity. Addictive and traumatic behaviors should be strongly discouraged. For instance, employees should not be expected to work—explicitly or implicitly—beyond the capacity of their job description; and gossip, blaming, and other disrespectful behaviors should never be tolerated.

Recovery requires a paradigm shift, individually and collectively. Treating the parasitic organization requires moving from a paradigm of competitive power to one of cooperative power. This paradigm shift won't occur just because you become aware of the problem; it will take a concerted effort to cultivate cooperative power on all levels of functioning. And it needs to be an ongoing process, one that is built into your organization's strategic plan. For instance, you could hold monthly evaluations of employee satisfaction and productivity and offer workshops on teambuilding, communication, and conflict resolution. Whatever the form your organization's efforts take to build cooperative power into the plan, one element is a must: staff should be educated about trauma and addictive behaviors, and they should be given resources to help them heal. I discuss recovery in greater depth in Chapter 9, in the context of self-care. (For further information see www.lanternbooks.com/resources.)

If you don't attend to your own sense of disempowerment, when faced with the magnitude of the abuse of power inherent in animal exploitation you may end up re-creating that which you are fighting. A strategic movement for animals is made up of strategic activists and organizations, and these depend on an ongoing commitment to personal and social empowerment.

Part III

＊

Strategic Activism
for Animals

8

✳

Stand and Deliver
Strategic Advocacy for Animals

You must become the change you wish to see in the world.
—Mahatma Gandhi

I ONCE OVERHEARD a conversation between a vegan and a curious meat eater at a dinner party. The meat eater, a man in his thirties, approached the vegan, a woman around the same age. The meat eater wanted to know how and why the vegan had stopped eating meat. The vegan, ideally poised to advocate, spent the next ten minutes rattling off all the reasons people shouldn't eat animals, angrily pointing out how much suffering was caused by meat eaters who "just didn't care" and proudly describing how much effort she put in to avoiding everything that contained animal products, including her clothing and shampoo. Of course, the meat eater was no longer curious, and worse, I later overheard him talking to someone about "those crazy vegans" and their "righteous self-denial." It's doubtless that any spark of openness to veganism the meat eater may have had was snuffed out that night. Why would he want to join a subculture made up of angry, self-centered, and deprived individuals?

Another example had a more positive outcome. A young female student of mine who was a vegan and peace activist used to sit next to a young man who was involved in human rights but hadn't made the connection between human and animal exploitation. The vegan often talked to the meat eater about human rights movements in which they were both active, and eventually started sharing her experience with animal rights. She was always careful to listen to the young man's questions about veganism, responding mostly by sharing her own experience ("For me, it was about making the connection between violence toward humans and violence toward animals...") and how she had been able to make the lifestyle change in a way that felt comfortable and empowering. Knowing that the man would feel uncomfortable coming to terms with his participation in animal exploitation, the vegan always validated his feelings by sharing how she, like many others, had also participated in practices that harmed animals because of a lack of awareness and the massive social pressure to maintain the status quo. Eventually the man became a supporter of animal rights due largely—if not entirely—to the fact that his first exposure to the issue was presented in a supportive, compassionate, and empowering manner by a person whose actions reflected these values.

My student was following the example of Mahatma Gandhi, who understood the most important principle of strategic advocacy: true change must begin with oneself. Though social transformation is never the result of the efforts of a single individual, great leaders can mobilize millions. And great leaders are, among other things, great advocates. Gandhi was able to wage a large-scale revolution for the first time in human history without picking up a single weapon.

Expectations and Advocacy

Whether your advocacy is effective or not depends largely on your expectations. Typically, people get what they *expect*, rather than what they *want*—from others and themselves—in a kind of self-fulfilling prophecy. One's expectations may not even be expressed consciously, but one way or another, they do get communicated, and others will often raise or lower themselves to meet these expectations. Consider how an underachieving student can rise to the top of the class simply because the teacher believes in her. Organizational scholars refer to this phenomenon as *expectancy theory*.

In terms of animal advocacy, many vegan advocates, for instance, sincerely want others to stop eating meat, but at the same time expect that the average person is too selfish or apathetic to truly change. They therefore resort to shaming and blaming. If you don't believe that others are sensitive and conscientious enough to change their behaviors, you will inevitably use forceful or manipulative tactics in an attempt to make them change. The antidote is to align your expectations with your desires and goals, so that what you expect is the same as what you want.

Developing Value-based Motives

Often activists *do* expect that their audience will be receptive to, for instance, veganism, assuming that any rational, humane person would not want to eat animals after learning of the brutality they suffer. Yet, more often than not the facts themselves don't sell the ideology. Many people learn about animal suffering and continue with their current lifestyle, for reasons we'll discuss later in this chapter. If you aren't prepared for this seemingly paradoxical response, and if the motives beneath your advocacy aren't pure, your attempts to promote your ideology may backfire.

In his best-selling book *The Seven Habits of Highly Effective People*, Stephen Covey says that "what we are communicates far more eloquently than what we do."[23] What Covey means is that our motivations and beliefs are transparent to others, even when our actions or speech seek to belie them. For instance, if a vegan who is advocating to a meat eater is motivated by a genuine concern for the other's well-being, the meat eater will feel more trusting, which will increase the likelihood that he or she will be receptive to the vegan's message. If, on the other hand, the vegan is simply motivated by the need to push his or her own agenda, the vegan will come across as manipulative, and will arouse the meat eater's defenses. Consider, for example, how it feels when a salesperson pitches a product without concern for your well-being. The salesperson may drip with sincerity and be full of enthusiasm, smiles, and promises, but will seem disingenuous all the while. Even if you believe that humankind would be better off if animal suffering were completely eliminated, this is a gross generalization that doesn't take into account the needs and perspective of the *individual* to whom you're advocating. You can't know what's in somebody else's best interests unless you truly listen to them and try to understand their *personal paradigm*.

Personal Paradigms

Each person has a particular lens through which he or she views the world. This *personal paradigm* is formed by the synthesis of one's values, assumptions, and life experiences. Even though people who have had similar experiences may have similar paradigms, no two paradigms are exactly alike. Because personal paradigms are naturally subjective, there's no "right" or objective way to view reality. So, for instance, a couple may live with a dog but disagree about whether to let the dog sleep with them. Each might find the other's perspective offensive: the partner who grew up sharing his bed with his dog might believe it's unethical not to allow the dog in the bed, while the partner whose family never had pets might find it unhygienic. Neither partner is "wrong;" each just sees the same situation differently.

It's easy to become wedded to a particular view, especially when the opposing one seems to endorse unethical practices. However, when activists have an inflexible paradigm—when, for instance, vegans see no ethical difference between the meat eating of peasants in Southeast Asia and that of wealthy Americans, they come across as rigid and dogmatic (and they also limit their own growth as individuals). If an activist is fervently promoting veganism without being open to others' perspectives, the audience will tend to focus on the *activist*, rather than the *issue*. Consider televangelists. Do you hear their message when they're on TV? They could be sharing the secrets of the universe but most people are too distracted by their manner to actually know what they're saying.

Another problem that arises from a "single approach" perspective is that you can fail to understand those to whom you are advocating. And knowing your audience is fundamental to strategic advocacy.

Know Your Audience

One of the most common mistakes activists make is assuming that information alone will change people's minds about animals. This assumption is made in regard to all forms of animal cruelty, but I'll again use meat eating as an example: vegans often think that once people realize the horrors of factory farming, they will no longer have any desire to eat meat. Their strategy for advocacy is therefore simply to present people with the truth about meat production. And when the listener responds with justifications for his or her meat eating, changes the subject, or agrees emphatically but continues to eat animals, the vegan is exasperated and resentful. Often during conversations about meat eating, the more resistant the listener is, the harder the vegan pushes, responding with *yes, buts,* and *what ifs*: "Yes, but we wouldn't have to worry about what to do with all the animals if everyone went vegetarian because we wouldn't be breeding them in the first place," and "What if you had to kill the animal yourself? Would you still be able to eat meat?" While it's important to respond to some of the meat eater's objections, it's more important to understand the reason for the objections in the first place. Most objections are in fact irrational, which is a clear indicator that they are driven by emotion rather than logic. *It is the emotion beneath the objections that should be the focus of the advocate.* Getting caught up in intellectual argumentation can distract from the heart of the issue.

My doctoral and post-doctoral research has focused on the reasons people support animal exploitation, specifically meat production. What I've found is that, because most people are deeply disturbed by and feel guilty about eating meat, and yet at the same time fear *not* eating it, they defend themselves from having to acknowledge such conflicting feelings. These *psychological defenses* include *denial* ("Animals don't really suffer when they're raised and killed for meat."); *justification* ("Animals are meant to be eaten by humans."); *dichotomization* ("I'd never eat a dog, but I love bacon."); *avoidance* ("Don't tell me that; you'll ruin my meal."); and, most importantly, *dissociation* ("If I think about the animal when I'm eating meat I feel disgusted.").

All defenses exist to support dissociation, or emotional disconnection. They defend against potentially painful feelings. When people break through their dissociation, the feelings that typically emerge are empathy—and therefore disgust. That's why people tend to be disgusted by the idea of eating "unusual" animals, such as dogs and gorillas; they haven't learned to dissociate from these kinds of meat. It's also why vegetarians usually find all meats disgusting.

As I mentioned, people fear not eating meat. In *Living Among Meat Eaters*, Carol Adams describes the fears people have about what might happen were they to stop eating animals: they could be ostracized from their friends and family; they could feel deprived; they could get sick or lose weight; they could feel overwhelmed by yet another issue to take on; they could be stereotyped and judged by society; they could lose their sense of innocence and safety when they realize they've been deceived by their family and society about the suffering of animals; they could feel deep guilt and sadness; and, most notably, they could lose their identity. These concerns may seem trivial to vegans, especially with regard to the plight of the animals being eaten, but they're anything but trivial to meat eaters. If activists don't respect meat eaters' fears, they won't be able to advocate effectively.

I have argued that meat eaters are strongly wedded to their identity, or paradigm, though most people—including vegetarians and vegans—don't realize it. I've maintained that, just as eating a vegetarian diet is an expression of an ideology, so is eating meat. But because meat eating is the dominant ideology, it hasn't been named. Its invisibility makes meat eating seem like a given, rather than a choice. I have named this ideology *carnism*, and refer to meat eaters as *carnists*. Asking people to stop eating meat is asking not just for a change in their behavior, but for a radical change in their identity when it comes to how they relate to other animals and to themselves. It's asking for a paradigm shift, a conversion of sorts, almost as if a Catholic were to try to convert a Jew to Christianity. Given these factors, it's no wonder carnists can get so defensive.

As with any dominant ideology, the carnistic system rewards conformity and punishes deviation. It's much easier to eat meat, practically and psychologically: those who give up meat are often negatively stereotyped, and they have to work harder to make sure their dietary needs are met. This pressure to conform fuels carnistic defenses. On top of this, carnistic industry actively encourages defenses by, for instance, using a picture of a happy pig dancing over a fire pit to sell pork, which distorts and obscures the reality of hog farms. Often, vegan advocates assume that a person's defensiveness is the result of selfishness or apathy, when in fact it is much more likely the result of systematic and intensive social conditioning.

Animal liberation activists need to break through such dissociation and challenge personal paradigms in a way that minimizes defensiveness. Because of the sensitivity people have to learning about animal suffering, particularly suffering that they've participated in through their choices as consumers, breaking through their dissociation is no small feat. Without an emotional safety net, the listener will be unlikely to hear your message.

Creating a Safety Net

Many people are highly defended against challenges to their personal paradigm. Personal paradigms are familiar, comfortable, and *safe*. Too much change too quickly can cause a backlash; if advocates aren't careful, they can end up reinforcing defenses and even exacerbating the assumptions and behaviors they are trying to transform. A common mistake is to inundate people with "the truth" without considering how this information will impact their perception of themselves and their world. Change is scary. People need to feel safe in order even to be open to the idea of change.

One way you can help listeners feel safe is to walk the fine line between *challenging* and *supporting* the listener's paradigm. You must challenge the parts you want to change while reinforcing the parts that support this change. For instance, if you're an anti-fur advocate, you could encourage people to question their support of the fur industry but affirm their willingness to think critically. You could say, "Here's the truth about fur, and I admire your openness to hearing what I know can be disturbing information." Personal paradigms have positive and negative aspects; when challenging the negative, highlight its positive counterpart.

People also feel safe when they feel accepted. The minute a person feels judged, he or she self-protectively shuts down.

Judgment causes shame, and shame is the feeling of being "less than," of being disempowered. Disempowered people withdraw or attack rather than open to information. To help people feel accepted, you have to listen empathically, and listen more than you speak. When the listener feels validated in his or her experience, he or she is much more likely to engage in productive dialogue. And you can make sure the dialogue is productive by focusing on the *process* of a conversation, rather than the *results*. The process is simply the way people are communicating. It can be receptive or defensive, clear or ambiguous, empathic or self-centered. The process must be empowering for the content, the message, to be received. The goal of a conversation should be to have authentic, compassionate dialogue, rather than to convert someone to a cause.

In order to establish a safe environment and an empowering conversational process, you also have to pay attention to the listener's and your own emotional responses. If the listener seems to be getting defensive, change the subject to something lighter, or back off from talking and give him or her more space to communicate. If you feel yourself starting to get defensive, try to understand why this is happening and take a break from the conversation if necessary. Consider whether the listener may be triggering a reaction in you because he or she reflects something within *you* that you're not comfortable with. We all have within ourselves the capacity for good and evil. In general, the qualities in ourselves that we can't accept are the same qualities we reject in others, and our defensiveness is triggered when they act these qualities out. For example, an activist who can't acknowledge that some of her actions harm others (it's impossible to live without causing some degree of suffering) might reject what she sees as others' hypocrisy. But, of course, if the listener is being disrespectful toward you, you always have the right to end the conversation.

Another way to create a safety net is to show your vulnerability and fallibility. When people's paradigms are challenged, they feel vulnerable and also at fault for having possibly been wrong in their assumptions. When the playing field is more level, however, it's easier for them to allow themselves to be open. If you are willing to share *your* "imperfections" and fears, the listener will feel more comfortable reflecting on his or her own. For instance, you could describe what it was like for you to learn about animal suffering, the guilt you felt when you discovered that you'd supported certain practices, and how you've realized that good people can support inhumane practices for many understandable reasons. As with any conversation, it's awkward when only one person discloses personal information or feelings, and a strategic advocate for animals creates an atmosphere that is as comfortable as possible.

Strategic Communication

Effective communication is essential for effective advocacy. An effective communicator is a person with whom listeners feel not only good, but good about *themselves*. Effective communicators are clear, direct, and sensitive when they speak and attentive when they listen. Following are tips for communicating about animal issues:

- Never present animal liberation as an all-or-nothing lifestyle, or it seems an impossible ideal rather than a practical series of behavioral shifts.

- Be willing to admit that you don't have all the answers.

- Though you can't have all the answers, it's useful to be prepared for as many questions as possible. You'll feel more confident and therefore be less likely to get defensive.

- Avoid too much debate. Often, discussions about animal suffering get derailed by intellectual parrying, which detracts from the real issue of one's personal contribution to animal exploitation. Some justifications need to be discussed or the conversation will get stalled, but don't let the conversation stay in the realm of the mind. *Knowing* may lay the groundwork for change, but *feeling* inspires action.

- Know when not to advocate. Pick your battles and don't waste time trying to persuade people who are the least likely to be open to what you have to say. Also, avoid discussing issues that are not practical; for instance, debating the ethics of hunting with an environmentalist isn't particularly useful since hunting is the least of the problems facing animals today.

- Find common ground. Finding something you have in common with the listener creates a connection and therefore an opening for dialogue.

- Frame problems proactively. Be solution- rather than problem-oriented.

- View conflict as normal and an opportunity to grow.

- Ask questions to understand your listener's particular concerns and motivations better.

- Don't advise. Avoid words such as *should* or *have to,* or people will feel controlled and become defensive.

- Use "I" statements and personal stories so people feel less blamed or preached at. For example, say, "I remember how, when I stopped eating meat, I was surprised by the number of vegetarian choices I had."

- Avoid loaded, provocative words, such as *flesh*, *torture*, and *murderer*.

- Keep your body language open (arms unfolded, legs uncrossed) and make eye contact.

- Let the other person know you're listening by reflecting back to him or her what was said. For example, say, "So, you're worried that if you stop eating meat it will cause conflict with your husband."

- Don't over-inform. People can only take in so much information at once.

- Don't use too many statistics. Large numbers are hard to grasp and rarely move people.

- Never compare suffering, arguing that animals suffer more than humans. Even if you believe this to be true, it's almost guaranteed to offend the listener.

- Don't discuss meat production when people are eating meat. They will be that much more uncomfortable and therefore more defensive.[24]

- Don't be too serious. Take the *issue* seriously, but *yourself* lightly. Keep a sense of humor.

- Don't ever insinuate that someone is a hypocrite for not supporting animal liberation. We are all hypocrites; it's not where we draw the line around our circle of compassion, but how we relate to it that counts.

- When it comes to meat, see carnists as victims rather than opponents.

- Accept that people only have so much time to devote to a cause and not everyone will prioritize animals. At the same time, point out that it's possible to work for other issues and not eat animals in the process.

Gandhi was a master advocate because he had both practical skills and personal integrity. A strategic advocate for animals must have these qualities as well, and must make an ongoing commitment to their continued development. In this way, you can become an agent of change for the animals, and for yourself.

9

*

Activism for Life
Why Strategic Activism Is Sustainable Activism

You can't describe it unless you've seen it.
You can't explain it unless you've done it.
You can't imagine it unless you've been there.
Then it never goes away.—Bill Blessington, Reporter

I USED TO volunteer for a feline rescue organization, helping to trap and rehabilitate stray and feral cats. While I was working there, I met another volunteer, who was one of the most dedicated activists I'd known. She had a full-time job as a cashier at a gas station, but in all her free time she rescued cats and worked on local animal rights campaigns for different organizations. There was nothing this woman wouldn't do for the animals. Whenever someone asked for her help with an animal-related issue, she was there—whether it was to take in another stray cat (she was already fostering ten in her home), leaflet at a demonstration in the frigid

Boston winter, or help organize a major anti-fur campaign. Her energy, commitment, and versatility amazed me.

When I met this activist, she had been volunteering for several years. She was chronically tired and often stressed, but that was to be expected, given the amount and type of activism she engaged in. Yet over time, her fatigue and stress morphed into exhaustion, frustration, and despair. She worried endlessly about the thousands of cats she knew were freezing in Boston alleyways, and hated the people responsible for causing this problem. She resented the fact that she was always the person who devoted weekends and evenings to working on animal rights campaigns, but felt unable to say no because she didn't want to let the animals down. She felt guilty and frivolous at the thought of spending an evening relaxing at home when so many animals were suffering. In fact, she felt guilty most of the time, no matter how many sacrifices she made: when she was lying in bed, she'd think about all the animals outside in the cold and when she was driving in her car, she'd think about the animals being transported to slaughter. Her demanding schedule left no time for fun or friends. Eventually, this activist who'd started out as a tireless champion for the animals became an embittered, weary, and depressed woman who quit the movement. I've always wondered how many more animals she could have saved if she'd taken care of herself.

Activism is like running a marathon: those who try to sprint the whole distance don't make it past the first quarter. Activist-sprinters crash and burn, and often take others with them. Their anger, despair, and exhaustion become toxic and spill out onto those around them. In their noble race to save animals, they sacrifice themselves and end up without the support they need—

internally and externally—to sustain them for the long haul. They wind up suffering from the very trauma they are fighting against, becoming victims rather than active agents of change.

As with preparing for a marathon, there are ways to train so that your activism is sustainable. Activists who appreciate their feelings and needs, recognize the symptoms of Secondary Traumatic Stress Disorder (STSD), get support from others, make self-care a priority, and know how to manage their time efficiently are more effective and happier in their work for the animals. Strategic activism is sustainable activism, and as with other strategic concepts, this can and should be learned.

If They Could See What We See

"Animal people" must constantly emotionally navigate situations that others take for granted. What to a meat eater looks like a mouth-watering hamburger, for instance, appears to a vegetarian as an amalgam of carcasses—a disturbing and disgusting sight. On top of this, the meat eater may be a close friend or relative of the vegetarian's. So not only does the vegetarian have to contend with the horror of being exposed to meat, he or she also has to reconcile the fact that a loved one is dining on the remains of an innocent animal just because it tastes good, and without even considering the vegetarian's feelings. The vegetarian has to hold contradictory feelings toward the meat eater: anger and revulsion at his or her behavior and love and respect for his or her humanity *beyond* the behavior. Coping with situations like this requires a certain degree of psychological gymnastics and causes tremendous emotional strain. When activists aren't aware of their mental and emotional reactions, they can suffer needlessly and find their activism compromised.

"Animal people" inhabit a vastly different world from others. When you become aware of the extent of animal suffering, there is almost nowhere that is safe from potentially traumatizing imagery: movies and television shows feature mistreated animals; clothing stores sell fur and leather; every food venue from gas-station convenience stores to wedding caterers offers cutlets, wings, jerky, and ribs; restaurants display tanks of live lobsters; trucks carry meat products or living animals; university science laboratories conduct vivisection; petting zoos at community fairs display goats and lambs; people kill fish in the lake at which you're trying to relax; children throw stones at seagulls on the beach; every corner of your office building houses a mousetrap; dead animals litter the side of the road; guests at a dinner party pass a roast around the table. The list is virtually endless. And all the while, the rest of society denies the suffering and resents the people who try to do something about it. While activists spend precious time and energy (and often money) trying to clean up the mess created by others, they are often ridiculed and derided for this. For instance, the activist who rescues abandoned cats is "the crazy cat lady" who supposedly keeps cats not because she genuinely cares about the welfare of others and is willing to sacrifice her own comfort to save lives, but because she can't manage a relationship with humans. An act of great compassion is instead portrayed as a symptom of psychopathology; were the victims human, this woman would be a hero.

Because traumatic triggers are ubiquitous, activists have got to develop *resiliency*—the ability to withstand traumatization. This is especially important for activists who are working on campaigns in which they have to witness cruelty toward animals. Witnesses to trauma who are not resilient end up becoming vic-

tims, and victims by definition are powerless to help themselves
or others. Personal empowerment is the antidote to victimization. And understanding and giving yourself the time and energy to process painful emotions is the first step toward becoming
empowered.

Healthy Feeling

Those who are aware of and sensitive to animal suffering will
inevitably feel anger, sadness, confusion, fear, and a sense of
betrayal by our society and species. These feelings are normal,
natural, and legitimate. They reflect empathy and the courage to
face painful realities in the face of significant pressure to conform to the status quo. In fact, a primary reason there is such
extensive animal suffering is because so many people *don't* feel
these emotions. However, when these feelings aren't properly
managed, they become toxic and turn activists from active witnesses into passive victims—or worse, perpetrators. The two
most problematic emotions for activists are anger and grief.
Unmanaged anger morphs into toxic rage and unprocessed grief
becomes despair. While healthy anger and organic grief motivate
people to work for change, rage and despair can be paralyzing.

Anger Management

Anger is a normal and healthful response to injustice and plays
a vital role in social movements by energizing and mobilizing
people to fight for change. It mitigates fear and fuels courage.
Productive anger is an emotional response to *a particular situation
or action*, and it usually subsides when the problem has been
resolved. Even when the problem is ongoing, as with animal
exploitation, productive anger stays focused on the issue and

doesn't spill over into other areas of one's life. Productive anger is directed toward a person's behavior, rather than his or her character.

There's a difference between being *angry*, and being an angry *person*. Toxic anger is chronic anger that's become part of one's identity. When activists overexpose themselves to suffering and underexpose themselves to forms of support that would offset the negative effects of their witnessing, their anger can turn to rage. Toxic anger leads activists to burn out, thwarts effective communication, reinforces the stereotype of the angry human-hater, and divides activists from one another. Angry people may not seem angry, but they often have characteristic beliefs, feelings, behaviors, and ailments that signal underlying anger. Some of these include:

- Feelings of agitation.
- The assumption that things should go "their way" and feelings of disappointment when they don't.
- Reactivity, lashing out at others.
- Excessive pessimism, hostility, cynicism, or sarcasm.
- Depression and lack of motivation.
- A self-righteous attitude.
- Physical symptoms, such as headaches, digestive problems, or insomnia.

Managing anger requires first and foremost an awareness of that anger and its cause. Becoming *emotionally self-aware* puts you in a position to attend to your emotions and the issue that caused them in the moment, rather than after they've mixed with other feelings and are removed from their source. For instance, if your supervisor tells you that because you're doing such a great job she's putting you in charge of another project, even though you've made it clear that you're already overwhelmed, you'll probably feel angry. You'll also be less likely to notice your anger, since your supervisor's disregard of your needs was masked by a compliment, and perhaps also because you wouldn't feel your anger is justified when so many animals are suffering and you've been given more of a chance to help them. So you stuff the feeling down. Over time, as this happens again and again, the anger grows, mixes with other emotions that you've repressed, and you end up chronically irritable and perhaps depressed without even knowing why.

Managing anger also requires that you allow yourself to express it assertively and proactively, rather than reactively, or aggressively. If, for example, you are in a situation like the one described above, faced with a supervisor who appears to disregard your needs, try to be on alert for signals that you are angry. Rather than blow up at your supervisor, which would probably just create more anger between the two of you, you should state that you're angry, and why, and be clear about what you need in order to feel the situation is rectified. Following are some techniques that can be helpful in managing anger:

- Try not to communicate when you're extremely angry. Calm down before addressing the problem.

- When possible, avoid situations that you know will anger you. Anger can become addictive and activists may be drawn to situations that will trigger it, so as to have an excuse to express some of their pent-up rage.

- Build breaks or "downtime" into your day so you don't overwork and become resentful.

- Avoid using black-and-white thinking and intensifying language such as *always*, *never*, *disaster*. For example, saying "He never does anything right" is inaccurate, as no person is in error one-hundred percent of the time; this attitude exaggerates the problem and fuels anger.

- Accept that not all problems have a solution and let go of what you can't control.

- Identify the "shoulds" or judgmental beliefs that underlie your anger. Try to be more accepting of others' value systems.

- Direct your anger at a person's actions, not his or her character. Anger often causes us to look at others with blinders, as though they are nothing more than a behavior or set of behaviors that we've judged as "bad" or "wrong." Instead, consider, for example, that the woman in the fur coat isn't a "selfish speciesist" but is someone's daughter, perhaps someone's mother or sister—she's someone who has fears and hopes, who feels vulnerable in the world and, like everyone, is doing her best to survive emotionally and physically. And maybe her coat was passed down from her deceased grandmother, or she's from a country where there's limited awareness about fur production.

- Feel your anger, but respond with compassion. It's not how you feel, but how you respond to your feelings that matters.

- Be prepared for provocative comments: when you're caught off-guard and can't defend yourself, you feel more helpless and therefore angrier. For example, if someone calls you a hypocrite for being vegetarian and wearing leather shoes, you can agree but say that you're doing your best to make a difference while still respecting your own comfort level. You can point out that just because you're not doing "everything," this doesn't mean you're doing nothing. Responding without anger can head off defensive debate and open up productive dialogue.

Despair Management

Despair is the feeling of hopelessness that results from holding in chronic grief or sadness. Despair can also emerge when you've been feeling frustrated and disempowered from not seeing the results of your efforts. Despair is the feeling that nothing will change.

The best antidote to despair is prevention: if you begin to feel grief and sadness, let it happen, let yourself feel and express your sadness in the moment. Activists often go to great lengths to avoid feeling their grief, fearing that if they open themselves to it, it will consume them and they'll be unable to continue with their activism. Activists say they "can't afford" to let themselves feel. The truth is, however, you can't afford *not* to let yourself feel. Giving yourself permission to feel grief is necessary in order to manage it. Also, you can head off despair by making sure that you choose projects or tasks that give you some sense of accomplishment. Avoid overworking, and avoid exposure to too much traumatizing material. Perhaps most importantly, accept the fact that there's much you cannot change.

Despair is an isolating feeling; people often feel alone in their despair. And in a vicious cycle, isolation typically exacerbates one's sense of disempowerment and traumatization. For this reason, if prevention fails and despair has set it in, turning to community can help. Sharing your despair with others can show you that you aren't alone in your struggle, and can help you feel witnessed in your sadness and frustration, validating your feelings. Many activists avoid sharing their despair, fearing they will be judged as inept or not committed enough. But with good support, whether it be another individual or a group, sharing despair can be mutually empowering and lift the burden of one person carrying so much sadness by themselves. Even if you don't share your despair with other activists, journaling about it, talking with a loved one, or simply letting yourself acknowledge it can have a healing effect.

Secondary Traumatic Stress Disorder (STSD)

When feelings are left to fester, they not only morph into destructive emotions, they can commingle and evolve into something even more serious: Secondary Traumatic Stress Disorder (STSD). STSD is like Post-traumatic Stress Disorder (PTSD) except that it comes from *witnessing* violence, rather than from being a direct victim. STSD is pervasive among activists, due to the nature and extent of animal cruelty they witness, the lack of social support for animal welfare, and the lack of awareness in activist organizations about the disorder.

STSD is not the same as Secondary Traumatic Stress (STS). While the symptoms are the same, STS is a normal, universal response to witnessing violence. STS only becomes a disorder when the symptoms haven't been properly managed over time. Some of the most common symptoms of STS/D include: frequent, intrusive recollections of the event(s); recurring nightmares of the event; loss of interest in significant activities; heightened anxiety; difficulty falling or staying asleep; oversleeping; a feeling of dissociation or detachment from oneself and others; feeling emotionally numb or emotionally hypersensitive; difficulty concentrating; and feeling guilty for not suffering as much as others, also known as *survivor guilt*.

Survivor Guilt

Survivor guilt is the guilt felt by those who survived a trauma that others did not. Like any unprocessed emotion, survivor guilt can become debilitating. If activists aren't aware that they're feeling survivor guilt, they may attempt to quell their discomfort in a number of destructive ways, including overworking and other forms of self-denial. Activists may channel their feelings into their work, distracting themselves from their emotional discomfort and in a sense punishing themselves for not suffering as others are. They work harder to feel less guilty about the animals they haven't been able to save, and feel undeserving of personal happiness in a world so full of violence. If you find yourself putting in longer hours and piling more work onto a large workload, think carefully about the source of your motivation.

Projection is another way unprocessed guilt expresses itself. Projection occurs when a person sees in others the feelings he or she refuses to acknowledge in him- or herself. Activists may deny their own guilt and project it onto others, making *them* feel guilty by judging, shaming, and blaming them.

You can manage your survivor guilt by recognizing it for what it is, and realizing that your own suffering will not reduce the suffering of others. In fact, if you *don't* attend to your own suffering, your activism won't be sustainable and you will save fewer animals than you could otherwise. You can also manage your survivor guilt by learning to accept the world as it is—while still working to improve it—and to be compassionate toward yourself in the process.

Sustainable Activism

Trauma is the result of violence. The core of trauma is disempowerment and disconnection.[25] Preventing and treating trauma therefore requires the opposite: empowerment and connection. Empowerment and connection depend on developing a cooperative way of relating to power. Activists need to cultivate a system of support, through developing healthful relationships, as they also learn to relate to their own selves compassionately. Empowerment is practicing nonviolence toward self and others.

Compassionate Witnessing

Compassionate witnessing[26] is the cornerstone of nonviolence. Compassionate witnessing is the act of bearing witness with empathy and compassion, and *without judgment.* When you are a compassionate witness, you are a truly present and focused listener. You don't try to "fix" someone's problem, turn away from someone's pain, or cheer someone up by distracting him or her from the situation. And you don't suggest someone is "overreacting" or remind someone that things could be worse, a truism activists are usually all too aware of, which is why their survivor guilt can be consuming. Rather, you validate that person's feelings and experience, and in so doing empower him or her tremendously. This same process works internally, as well. When you act as a compassionate witness to your own feelings and thoughts, you empower yourself.

External Supports

Trauma isolates; resiliency requires community. Animal liberation activists live in a world where their core values and experience are systematically denied, minimized, and violated. This is isolating and disempowering. Activists are also isolated on a practical level, knowing that they'll likely be on their own if they stop to help a hurt animal or speak out against animal cruelty. Therefore, creating a system of support among other activists can be extremely valuable.

Starting an Activist Support Group

Support groups have been highly effective for helping trauma survivors heal and develop resiliency. For activists, support groups can create solidarity, provide a safe place to witness one another, and help cultivate new relationships with like-minded people. The despair, guilt, and isolation that activists so commonly feel can dissolve as the group affirms and legitimizes their experiences. Members can also share their own techniques for managing difficult emotional and practical situations and therefore learn from one another.

Anyone can form an activist support group. I highly recommend structuring a group around the Twelve-Step model. This model has been around for many years and is known to be effective. It was created specifically to prevent dysfunctional group dynamics (which are otherwise almost impossible to avoid) and to cultivate greater personal empowerment. Ideal for managing secondary traumatic stress, Twelve-Step groups function largely as compassionate witnessing circles, while the steps provide a framework for practicing cooperative power. The main criticism of the Twelve-Step model is its focus on spirituality. However, many people have adapted the program so that its definition of spirituality fits in with their own paradigm, even for those who are atheist.

Starting a Local Animal Emergency Network

I was once on my way to an important job interview when I

found a lost dog darting in and out of traffic. I was faced with a terrible choice: stop and help the dog and miss my interview, or continue on my way and hope the dog didn't get hit by a car. I chose to help the dog, but at great personal expense. Had there been a network of activists to call on, I wouldn't have had to face the situation alone.

A local animal emergency network is a group of animal-friendly people who have agreed to offer support in an emergency. The agreement doesn't mean the group members have to drop everything to respond to a crisis; it means they are willing to be called, and will help if and when they are able. To start an emergency animal network, you need to compile a calling tree and ideally an e-mail list of everyone in the area who can be a resource. People can specify what kind of support they can offer: providing a car for transport; offering temporary shelter; funding medical expenses; keeping an updated list of emergency services, such as shelters and veterinary hospitals; helping make decisions, such as whether to call animal control; and helping with the direct rescue. People should specify what their availability is (e.g., no calls after midnight) and what their other limits are. Individuals should *never* be asked to go beyond what they offer or the network will be unsustainable. Animal emergency networks can connect people who care about animals, help reduce activists' stress, and make it possible to save more animals.

Creating a Resilient Organization

All too often, activist organizations either fail to cultivate resiliency among staff, or actively work against it, as is the case with power parasites that I discussed in Chapter 7. Parasitic organizations are traumatic, while cooperative organizations are empowering. Organizations can do a great deal to ensure that staff is resilient. One way is to build awareness of STSD into the organization. Organizations can ensure that new staff, particularly those in leadership positions, learn about STSD, and that informational materials are available at all times. Other methods are as follows:

- Not allowing staff to overwork, at least not so much that it becomes a pattern of behavior.
- Giving staff projects that yield tangible results, to mitigate the sense of helplessness.
- Allowing for the expression of feelings.
- Celebrating all victories, no matter how small.
- Recognizing individual members' successes.
- Holding weekly meetings for staff to discuss their experience of STS.

Supporting Your Self
Self-deprivation is a way of life for many activists. One reason is because, out of survivor guilt, activists deny their needs and desires, feeling they don't deserve fulfillment when so many animals are suffering. But many activists are deprived because their efforts to save animals leave them with limited incomes and very little free time. Thus, one of the most important factors in developing resiliency is maintaining effective self-care. Following are guidelines for taking care of yourself so you can have a healthful, fulfilling, and sustainable activist career:

- Try to interact with healthy, happy animals when possible.

Having tangible experiences of happy animals offsets images of animal suffering.

- Choose forms of activism that feel comfortable to you. Don't, for example, force yourself to work in a shelter if the thought of animals in cages is too upsetting. There are many ways to be active. Cater to your strengths and respect your limitations.

- Pay attention to traumatic triggers, and avoid them. Don't expose yourself to material that you know will traumatize you.

- Cultivate healthful relationships with people who aren't activists, to become more balanced and have a broader support system.

- Join a non-activist support group to help you deal with emotional issues.

- Take care of your body with exercise, proper nutrition, and adequate sleep. A weakened body makes you more susceptible to traumatization.

- Make sure you have fun every day, or at least several times a week.

- Find a form of creative expression that you enjoy. This can help you focus your attention away from traumatic memories and channel your energy into something productive.

- Develop skills to help you feel more effective and confident. For instance, you can take an assertiveness-training, communication-skills, or time-management workshop.

- Cultivate a spiritual practice, whatever spirituality means to you.

- Develop a time-management strategy so you don't end up bogged down by work. An excellent resource is Stephen Covey's *The Seven Habits of Highly Effective People*.

- Set goals for yourself outside of your activism, and develop a strategic plan to meet them.
- If you feel depressed, anxious, or chronically irritable, you may want to consider getting professional help. Therapy and/or medication can alleviate the vast majority of emotional problems.

Avoid Shame and Grandiosity

Shame is the feeling of having less power than you actually do; it's the core emotion of disempowerment. Shame is feeling "less than" or "one down." Grandiosity also stems from disempowerment, but it's the opposite of shame; it's feeling "better than" or "one up." Both of these feelings are self-destructive, and can hurt others as well.

Widespread ignorance of animal suffering, the devaluing of emotional sensitivity, and contradictions between people's beliefs and behaviors (loving their dogs while eating pigs), are trademarks of U.S. culture. Many Americans, when faced with someone who makes them aware of animal suffering, can respond with ignorance, defensiveness, or both. If you're in a situation like this, it's easy to react by feeling either grandiose or ashamed. Grandiosity is often expressed as self-righteousness and it can lead you to act in ways that disconnect you from others and that lower your self-regard.

Shame can make you question the validity of your feelings, but rather than rigidly defend them as you would if you were grandiose, you start to believe what others say about you. For example, if you're called a hypocrite for eating eggs but not meat you might feel guilty and hypocritical; if you're told you're over-reacting to a situation involving what you perceive as animal cruelty, you might believe that you're hypersensitive. Or, if you're called "fussy" because you won't eat pasta sauce after the meatballs have been picked out, you might feel like you're too picky.

It's important not to internalize critical, negative messages about yourself. You can prevent feeling ashamed by applying some of the principles of personal empowerment discussed in this book, and also by becoming informed about the issues that shame you. For example, your reaction to the "tainted" pasta sauce would be no different from the reaction of a meat eater whose sauce had contained meatballs made of dogs. Disgust, which is what you would have felt, is considered by psychologists to be a "moral emotion." It's an aversion to eating something that a person finds morally inappropriate. And disgust has "contamination properties," which means that whatever touches the disgusting object becomes "tainted" or disgusting as well. In other words, your reaction to the pasta sauce was a *bona fide*, normal psychological response, and knowing this can be tremendously empowering.

Cultivating a sustainable life as an activist takes commitment, patience, and courage. Resiliency develops over time, but the work is well worth the effort. Sustainable activism enables you to have a more fulfilling and healthful life and ultimately to help more animals. As Buddhist and activist Thich Nhat Hanh says, one must *be* peace in order to truly work for peace.

10

*

Conclusion
*Where Do We Go from Here? Evolving Strategy
for a Growing Movement*

*The dream of yesterday is the hope of today and the reality of
tomorrow.*—Robert Goddard

THE ABOVE QUOTE speaks to the heart of many animal liberation
activists. And strategy is the bridge between dreams and reality;
strategy is what turns the hope of today into the reality of
tomorrow. The purpose of this book is to help you realize your
dream of animal liberation.

Throughout this book, I have discussed how you can more
effectively work toward making the world a better place for animals, by implementing strategy on all levels: movement building,
organizing, and activism. We have examined how social movements evolve and win; the difference between animal liberation
and human liberation movements and how this impacts animal

advocacy; the divide–and–conquer counterstrategy that makes the movement kill itself; how to maintain a strategic organization and run strategic campaigns; why and how to start your own animal liberation organization; how to be a strategic advocate for animals; and how to make sure your activism is sustainable. There is, however, a final aspect of strategy that is important to understand: strategy either *evolves* or *expires*.

Strategic Development

Strategy is *relational*, in that it exists only in relation to the circumstances in which it has been developed. It is a reaction to a situation that in turn brings about another reaction, and so forth. If you were playing chess, you would choose your move depending on how your pieces stood in relation to each other, and to your opponent. And your choice would determine how your opponent reacted. With each move, the circumstances of the game change and you have to adapt your strategy accordingly. Your strategy must evolve, or it will no longer be useful.

Activists must make a commitment to having ongoing conversations about building the future of the movement in order to continue strategic development. Since the most powerful strategies are the result of collaborative effort, resulting from the combination of diverse perspectives and experiences, the most strategic action you can take is to commit to cooperative strategizing. You must nurture and share your strategies, so that they evolve rather than expire. Following are some of my suggestions for ways to foster strategic development:

Create a Web-based, Umbrella Animal Liberation Organization
A virtual umbrella organization would unite animal liberation

organizations and activists without centralizing power. Its purpose would be to serve as a database for the movement, and it could perform the following functions:

- List current animal liberation organizations, giving a brief description of who they are, how to contact them, and what they're doing. List the organizations' current and past campaigns and, if possible, their strategic campaign plans. By knowing what others have done and what their strategy was, activists can pool resources by, for instance, collaborating on existing campaigns and learning from past campaigns. Imagine, for example, if you wanted to start a campaign against your local fur distributor and you had access to another organization's research and strategic campaign plan.
- Host a bulletin board that covers a variety of topics, such as current events in the movement, legislative issues, and strategy. For instance, when new legislation is passed in a state, it could be posted on the board, along with an explanation of how activists were able to bring it about.
- Offer a question-and-answer bulletin on issues ranging from how to rescue feral cats to how to run a petition drive.
- Create a discussion board for topics such as Secondary Traumatic Stress and strategic development.
- Distribute online petitions. Activists working on a petition drive could distribute their petitions through the Web site.
- Host cyber chats so that activists from different regions can meet each other.
- Post a calendar listing major events and news in animal liberation.
- Dedicate a portion of the site for activists from other move-

ments to participate in discussions and chats. For instance, there could be an area for Animals and the Environment or Animals and Feminism.

Conduct Market Research

In Chapter 4, I discussed how important it is to tailor outreach methods for specific target groups. In order to know how to tailor your message, you need to know what methods work for each group. The animal liberation movement as a whole still doesn't have answers to some important questions. For instance: Are people more or less likely to respond to graphic imagery? How much imagery is too much? Do women and men respond to the same images and arguments? Do teenagers respond to different forms of media than adults?

There is already some excellent work being done on market research; the Humane Research Council was developed specifically for this purpose. However, market research should be a priority across the movement. For example, professional opposition organizations that haven't already done so could start a department in their respective organizations for market research on their particular issue.

Develop Strategy Think Tanks

Think tanks are groups of people who come together to share their ideas and develop new ones. Strategy think tanks could be Web-based, as part of the umbrella organization, or you could start one in your community. Larger organizations should consider developing a division specifically for strategic development.

Develop and/or Participate in Strategic Trainings

A number of organizations that train activists in strategy already exist. Even though these trainings are not tailored specifically for animal liberation activists, they can be extremely beneficial. Animal liberation organizations could either send their staff to these trainings or develop their own trainings, which they could offer to their staff, members, and other activists.

Start a Local Support Group for Activists

I discussed the importance of support groups in Chapter 9. Starting your own group could be extremely beneficial, as you would have somewhere to discuss issues that you might not be able to share with others. Groups also connect activists and create a sense of community. Your group could be formal or informal, focused on Secondary Traumatic Stress or another specific issue, led by a designated organizer, or structured around the Twelve-Step model.

Continue Learning

Understanding and developing strategy is a lifelong process. You should continue to educate yourself in any area in which you feel you need to learn more, from grassroots fundraising to effective leadership.

Animal liberation may still be only a dream today. But with your courage, conviction, and commitment you can make it the reality of tomorrow. You can help make tomorrow a better day for animals.

Notes

✳

1. Arthur Ward, author, pastor, and teacher.
2. Marcus, *Meat Market*. See the Bibliography for full citation for this and other titles.
3. Moyer, *et al. Doing Democracy*.
4. Lakey, *Strategizing for a Living Revolution*, 99.
5. Foley, *Learning in Social Action*.
6. Singer, *Animal Liberation*.
7. Marcus, *Meat Market*.
8. Kaner, *et al. Facilitator's Guide to Participatory Decision-Making*.
9. Bobo, *et al. Organizing for Social Change*.
10. *Ibid*.
11. *Ibid*.
12. *Ibid*.
13. Jasper and Nelkin, *The Animal Rights Crusade*.
14. Bellaccomo, *Move the Message*. Several of the suggestions in this list are from her work.
15. *Ibid*.
16. Alinsky. *Rules for Radicals*.
17. Bobo, *et al. Organizing for Social Change*.
18. Bellaccomo, *Move the Message*.
19. Bobo, *et al*.

20. Bellaccomo, *Move the Message*.
21. *Ibid*.
22. Argyris, "Skilled Incompetence." *Harvard Business Review*, 74.
23. Covey. *The Seven Habits of Highly Effective People*, 22.
24. Adams, *Living Among Meat Eaters*.
25. Herman, *Trauma and Recovery*.
26. Weingarten, *Common Shock*.

Bibliography

＊

Adams, Carol J. "Feeding on Grace: Institutional Violence, Christianity, and Vegetarianism." *Good News for Animals? Christian Approaches to Animal Well-Being*. Eds. Charles Pinches and Jay B. McDaniel. Maryknoll, N.Y.: Orbis, 1993. 142–159.

_____. *Living Among Meat Eaters: The Vegetarian's Survival Handbook*. New York: Three Rivers Press, 2001; Continuum, 2003.

_____. *The Sexual Politics of Meat: A Feminist-Vegetarian Critical Theory*. New York: Continuum, 1992.

Adams, Carol and Josephine Donovan, eds. *Animals and Women: Feminist Theoretical Explorations*. Durham, NC: Duke University Press, 1995.

Albert, Michael. *The Trajectory of Change: Activist Strategies for Social Transformation*. Boston: South End Press, 2002.

Alinsky, Saul D. *Rules for Radicals: A Pragmatic Primer for Realistic Radicals*. New York: Vintage Books, 1971.

Allport, Gordon W. *The Nature of Prejudice*. New York: Addison-Wesley, 1958.

Argyris, Chris. "Skilled Incompetence." *Harvard Business Review* Sept.–Oct. 1986: 74.

Arluke, Arnold, and Clinton R. Sanders. *Regarding Animals*. Philadelphia: Temple University Press, 1996.

Bellaccomo, Josephine. *Move the Message: Your Guide to Making a Difference and Changing the World*. New York: Lantern Books, 2004.

Bly, Robert. "The Long Bag We Drag Behind Us." *Meeting the Shadow: The Hidden Power of the Dark Side of Human Nature*. Eds. Connie Zweig and Jeremiah Abrams. New York: Putnam, 1991. 6–12.

Bobo, Kim, Jackie Kendal, and Steve Max. *Organizing for Social Change: The Midwest Academy Manual for Activists*. 3rd ed. Santa Ana, Calif.: Seven Locks Press, 2001.

Boice, Judith. L. *The Art of Daily Activism*. Oakland, Calif.: Wingbow Press, 1992.

Bullard, Robert. D. *Confronting Environmental Racism: Voices from the Grassroots*. Boston: South End Press, 1993.

Clarke, Paul. A. B., and Andrew Linzey, eds. *Political Theory and Animal Rights*. London: Pluto Press, 1990.

Covey, Stephen. M. R., Stephen R. Covey, and Rebecca R. Merrill, R. R. *The Speed of Trust: The One Thing that Changes Everything*. New York: Free Press, 2006.

Covey, Stephen. R. *The Seven Habits of Highly Effective People: Powerful Lessons in Personal Change*. New York: Fireside, 1990.

Fiddes, Nick. *Meat: A Natural Symbol*. New York: Routledge, 1991.

Finsen, Lawrence and Susan Finsen. *The Animal Rights Movement in America: From Compassion to Respect*. New York: Twayne Publishers, 1994.

Flanagan, Joan. *The Grassroots Fundraising Book: How to Raise Money in Your Community*. Chicago: Contemporary Books, 1982.

Foley, Griff. *Learning in Social Action: A Contribution to Understanding Informal Education*. New York: Zed Books, 1999.

Fox, Michael. W. *Bringing Life to Ethics: Global Bioethics for a Humane Society*. Albany, N.Y.: State University of New York Press, 2001.

Francione, Gary. *Animals, Property, and the Law*. Philadelphia: Temple University Press, 1995.

_____. *Rain without Thunder: The Ideology of the Animal Rights Movement.* Philadelphia: Temple University Press, 1996.

Gardner, Howard. *Changing Minds: The Art and Science of Changing Our Own and Other People's Minds.* Boston: Harvard Business School Press, 2004.

Garner, Robert, ed. *Animal Rights: The Changing Debate.* New York: New York University Press, 1996.

Greenspan, Miriam. *Healing through the Dark Emotions: The Wisdom of Grief, Fear, and Despair.* Boston: Shambhala, 2003.

Hargrove, Eugene. C., ed. *The Animal Rights/Environmental Ethics Debate: The Environmental Perspective.* Albany, N.Y.: State University of New York Press, 1992.

Hawthorne, Mark. *Striking at the Roots: A Practical Guide to Animal Activism.* Berkeley, Calif.: O Books, 2008.

Herman, Judith. *Trauma and Recovery: The Aftermath of Violence—From Domestic Abuse to Political Terror.* New York: Basic Books, 1997.

Holmes, Robert. L. *Nonviolence in Theory and Practice.* Prospect Heights, Ill.: Waveland Press, 2001.

Horwitz, Claudia. *The Spiritual Activist: Practices to Transform Your Life, Your Work, and Your World.* New York: Penguin, 2002.

Ingram, Catherine. *In the Footsteps of Gandhi: Conversations with Spiritual Social Activists.* Berkeley, Calif.: Parallex Press, 1990.

Jasper, James M., and Dorothy Nelkin. *The Animal Rights Crusade: The Growth of a Moral Protest.* New York: Free Press, 1992.

Johnson, Allan. G. *Privilege, Power and Difference.* Mountain View, Calif.: Mayfield Publishing, 2001.

jones, pattrice. *Aftershock: Confronting Trauma in a Violent World, A Guide for Activists and Their Allies.* New York: Lantern Books, 2008.

Joy, Melanie. "From Carnivore to Carnist: Liberating the Language of Meat." *Satya* Sept. 2001: 26–27.

_____. "Psychic Numbing and Meat Consumption: The Psychology of

Carnism." Diss. Saybrook Graduate School, 2002. Ann Arbor: UMI, 2003.

Juergensmeyer, Mark. *Gandhi's Way: A Handbook of Conflict Resolution.* Berkeley: University of California Press, 2002.

Kaner, Sam, et al. *Facilitator's Guide to Participatory Decision-Making.* British Columbia, Canada: New Society Publishers, 1996.

Kapleau, Philip. *To Cherish All Life: A Buddhist Case for Becoming Vegetarian.* Rochester, N.Y.: The Zen Center, 1986.

Kaufman, Cynthia. *Ideas for Action: Relevant Theory for Radical Change.* Cambridge, Mass.: South End Press, 2003.

Kehler, Randall, Andrea Ayvazian, and Ben Senturia. *Thinking Strategically: A Primer on Long-range Strategic Planning for Grassroots Peace and Justice Organizations.* Amherst, Mass.: Exchange Project, Peace Development Fund.

Kinney, Jean. *Loosening the Grip: A Handbook of Alcohol Information.* 8th ed. New York: McGraw-Hill, 2006.

Lakey, George. *Strategizing for a Living Revolution.* New York: Institute for World Order, 1973.

Larsen, Earnie. *Stage II Recovery: Life Beyond Addiction.* San Francisco: Harper and Row, 1985.

Lifton, Robert. J. *The Nazi Doctors: Medical Killing and the Psychology of Genocide.* New York: Basic Books, 1986.

Macy, Joanna. "Working through Environmental Despair." *Ecopsychology: Restoring the Earth, Healing the Mind.* Eds. Allen D. Kanner, Theodore Roszak, and Mary E. Gomes. San Francisco: Sierra Club Books, 1995. 240–259.

Manheim, Jarol. B. *The Death of a Thousand Cuts: Corporate Campaigns and the Attack on the Corporation.* Mahwah, N.J.: Lawrence Erlbaum Associates, 2001.

Marcus, Erik. *Meat Market: Animals, Ethics, and Money.* Ithaca, N.Y.: Brio Press, 2005.

_____. *Vegan: The New Ethics of Eating.* Ithaca, N.Y.: McBooks, 1998.

Maurer, Donna. *Vegetarianism: Movement or Moment?* Philadelphia: Temple University Press, 2002.

Maxwell, John C., and Jim Dornan. *Becoming a Person of Influence: How to Positively Impact the Lives of Others.* Nashville, Tenn.: Nelson Business, 1997.

Mellody, Pia, Andrea Wells Miller, and Keith Miller. *Facing Codependence: What It Is, Where It Comes from, How It Sabotages Our Lives.* New York: HarperOne, 1989.

Merton, Thomas, ed. *Gandhi on Nonviolence: A Selection from the Writings of Mahatma Gandhi.* New York: New Directions, 1965.

Midgley, Mary. *Animals and Why They Matter: A Journey around the Species Barrier.* New York: Penguin Books, 1983.

Moyer, Bill, et al. *Doing Democracy: The MAP Model for Organizing Social Movements.* British Columbia, Canada: New Society Publishers, 2001.

Nibert, David. *Animal Rights/Human Rights: Entanglements of Oppression and Liberation.* Lanham, Md.: Rowman & Littlefield, 2002.

Norberg-Hodge, Helena. "Compassion in the Age of the Global Economy." *The Psychology of Awakening: Buddhism, Science, and Our Day-to-day Lives.* Eds. Gay Watson, Stephen Batchelor, and Guy Claxton. York Beach, Me.: Samuel Weiser, 2000. 55–67.

Oppenheimer, Martin, and George Lakey. *A Manual for Direct Action: Strategy and Tactics for Civil Rights and All Other Nonviolent Protest Movements.* Chicago: Quadrangle Books, 1965.

Pasick, Robert. *Awakening from the Deep Sleep: A Powerful Guide for Courageous Men.* San Francisco: HarperSanfrancisco, 1992.

Plous, Scott. "Psychological Mechanisms in the Human Use of Animals." *Journal of Social Issues* 49.1 (1993): 11–52.

Regan, Tom. *The Case for Animal Rights.* Berkeley, Calif.: University of California Press, 1983.

Rifkin, Jeremy. *Beyond Beef: The Rise and Fall of the Cattle Culture.* New York: Plume, 1992.

Robbins, John. *Diet for a New America*. Tiburon, Calif.: H. J. Kramer, 1987.

Rosen, Steven. *Diet for Transcendence: Vegetarianism and the World Religions*. Badger, Calif.: Torchlight Publishing, 1997.

Rozin, Paul, Maureen Markwith, and Caryn Stoess. "Moralization and Becoming a Vegetarian: The Transformation of Preferences into Values and the Recruitment of Disgust." *Psychological Science* 8.2 (1997): 67–73.

Saakvitne, Karen. W., and Laurie Anne Pearlman. *Transforming the Pain: A Workbook on Vicarious Traumatization*. New York: W. W. Norton, 1996.

Salzman, Jason. *Making the News: A Guide for Activists and Nonprofits*. Boulder, Colo.: Westview Press, 2003.

Schaef, Anne W., and Diane Fassel, D. *The Addictive Organization*. San Francisco: HarperCollins, 1988.

Schultz, Jim. "Strategy Development: Key Questions for Developing an Advocacy Strategy." The Democracy Center. Nov. 2008. www.democracyctr.org/library/advocacy/strategy.htm.

Schutt, Randy. *Inciting Democracy: A Practical Proposal for Creating a Good Society*. Cleveland, Ohio: Spring Forward Press, 2001.

Schwartz, Richard. H. *Judaism and Vegetarianism*. New York: Lantern Books, 2001.

Scully, Matthew. *Dominion: The Power of Man, the Suffering of Animals, and the Call to Mercy*. New York: St. Martin's Griffin, 2002.

Sen, Rinku. *Stir It Up: Lessons in Community Organizing and Advocacy*. San Francisco: Jossey-Bass, 2003.

Serpell, James. *In the Company of Animals*. New York: Basil Blackwell, 1986.

Sharp, Gene. *The Methods of Nonviolent Action*. Boston: Extending Horizons Books, 1973.

Shaw, Randy. *The Activist's Handbook*. Berkeley: University of California Press, 2001.

Shields, Katrina. *In the Tiger's Mouth: An Empowerment Guide for Social Action*. 1991. Victoria, Australia: Katrina Shields, 2000.

Singer, Peter. *Animal Liberation*. New York: Avon Books, 1990.

_____. *Ethics into Action: Henry Spira and the Animal Rights Movement*. Lanham, Md.: Rowman & Littlefield, 1998.

Spencer, Colin. *The Heretic's Feast: A History of Vegetarianism*. Hanover, N.H.: University Press of New England, 1995.

Spiegel, Marjorie. *The Dreaded Comparison: Human and Animal Slavery*. New York: Mirror Books, 1988.

Stamm, B. Hudnall, ed. *Secondary Traumatic Stress: Self-care Issues for Clinicians, Researchers, and Educators*. 2nd ed. Baltimore: Sidran Press, 1999.

Staples, Lee. *Roots to Power: A Manual for Grassroots Organizing*. 2nd ed. Westport, Conn.: Praeger Publishers, 2004.

Sun Tzu. *The Art of War*. Trans. Thomas Cleary. Shambala: Boston, 1991.

Thich Nhat Hanh. *Anger: Wisdom for Cooling the Flames*. New York: Riverhead Books, 2001.

_____. *For a Future to Be Possible: Commentaries on the Five Wonderful Precepts*. Berkeley: Parallax Press, 1993.

Twerski, Abraham. J. *Addictive Thinking: Understanding Self-Deception*. 2nd ed. Center City, Minn.: Hazelden Foundation, 1997.

Weingarten, Kaethe. *Common Shock: Witnessing Violence Every Day*. New York: NAL, 2004.

Weston, Anthony. *A Rulebook for Arguments*. 2nd ed. Indianapolis: Hackett Publishing, 1992.

Wise, Steven M. *Rattling the Cage: Toward Legal Rights for Animals*. Cambridge, Mass.: Perseus Publishing, 2000.

Workman, Dave P. *Peta Files: The Dark Side of the Animal Rights Movement*. Bellevue, Wa.: Merrill Press, 2003.

Appendices

✳

Appendix 1: Spectrum of Allies★

The Spectrum of Allies is a tool to help you decide which groups are most and least likely to support your organization or campaign, and which groups fall in the middle. The idea is to reach out to the groups that are closest to you and not waste time trying to convert the groups that are most resistant to your demand. With every group whose support you win over, you shift each wedge of the pie toward you and away from your opponent. The Spectrum of Allies demonstrates that you don't need to garner the support of all groups to shift the balance of power in your favor. It can also help you clarify the different constituencies you can reach out to, so that you can tailor your message appropriately. And remember: your opponent is likely creating a similar analysis and it would be helpful to consider what that one might look like as well.

First you need to clarify your goal. Then, brainstorm all the groups that have the potential to affect whether you attain your

---

★ Oppenheimer, Martin, and George Lakey. *A Manual for Direct Action: Strategy and Tactics for Civil Rights and All Other Nonviolent Protest Movements*. Chicago: Quadrangle Books, 1965. See http://trainingforchange.org/content/view/69/39/

goal. Once you've done this, put them in order of most and least resistant to supporting you on the pie chart. When you're done, you can make a plan about how to reach out to the group that's closest to you. Below is a sample diagram.

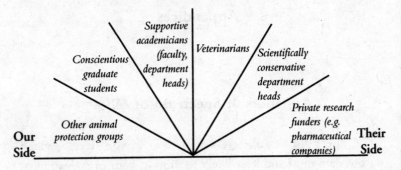

SPECTRUM OF ALLIES

Goal: Getting medical and veterinary schools to allow students to opt out of animal experiments

Appendix 2: Force Field Analysis★

A Force Field Analysis helps you clarify and weigh the pros and cons of an issue, such as an organizational goal or a campaign demand. It does this by helping you determine which forces are working for and against your objective, and how powerful each force is. The idea is to increase the forces working for you, and decrease the forces that are against you.

The first step is clearly stating your goal. Write this in the middle of the diagram. Then, on either side, list the forces for and against your goal. You should also assign a score to each of them, on a scale of 1–5, based on how powerful they are. You may also want to draft a diagram that you imagine represents your opponent's goal and forces, to better understand the opposition's perspective and possible course of action. A sample diagram is below.

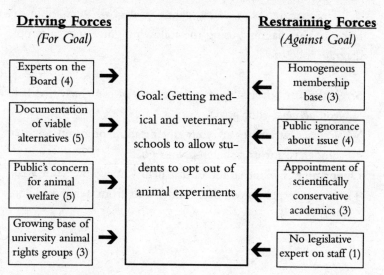

Driving Forces
(For Goal)

Experts on the Board (4)	→
Documentation of viable alternatives (5)	→
Public's concern for animal welfare (5)	→
Growing base of university animal rights groups (3)	→

Goal: Getting medical and veterinary schools to allow students to opt out of animal experiments

Restraining Forces
(Against Goal)

←	Homogeneous membership base (3)
←	Public ignorance about issue (4)
←	Appointment of scientifically conservative academics (3)
←	No legislative expert on staff (1)

★ The Force Field Analysis was created by Kurt Lewin.

Appendix 3: SWOT Analysis

A SWOT Analysis helps you determine the Strengths, Weaknesses, Opportunities, and Threats that pertain to your organization or campaign demand. You can use a SWOT Analysis after you've done a Force Field Analysis; the SWOT Analysis separates the information into *internal* and *external* issues. *Internal* issues refer to the strengths and weaknesses of your organization or campaign, and *external* issues are opportunities and threats from the outside that affect your organization or campaign. The idea is to clarify and increase your strengths and minimize your weaknesses. Ideally, you would also convert you weaknesses into strengths. And remember that your opposition is probably doing the same analysis, so you should consider what their chart would look like as well.

The first step is to clearly define your goal. Next, fill in the boxes of the diagram, using the following guidelines (a sample diagram follows):

Strengths: attributes of your organization or campaign that help you achieve your goal.

Weaknesses: attributes of your organization or campaign that hinder you from achieving your goal.

Opportunities: external forces that help you achieve your goal.

Threats: external forces that hinder you from achieving your goal.

	STRENGTHS	WEAKNESSES
INTERNAL	• MDs who are former vivisectors on Board • Documentation of viable humane alternatives • Documentation of cruelty in animal experiments	• Disagreements and conflicts around campaign plan • Homogeneous member base • No legislative expert on staff
	OPPORTUNITIES	THREATS
EXTERNAL	• Natural public concern for animal welfare • Growing base of universities that allow students to opt out of animal research • Growing base of university animal rights groups	• Public ignorance about the issue • Appointment of scientifically conservative academic officers

Of Related Interest from Lantern Books

＊

Andrew Beath
Consciousness in Action
The Power of Beauty, Love, and Courage in a Violent Time

Josephine Bellaccomo
Move the Message
Your Guide to Making a Difference and Changing the World

pattrice jones
Aftershock
Confronting Trauma in a Violent World
A Guide for Activists and Their Allies

Norm Phelps
The Longest Struggle
Animal Advocacy from Pythagoras to PETA

Hillary Rettig
The Lifelong Activist
How to Change the World without Losing Your Way